Praise for
Everyday Courage for Schoo.

Leadership is about fostering growth, building capacity, and collaboratively working with stakeholders to create new ideas—this takes a great deal of courage. Cathy Lassiter creates a pathway for leaders to develop that courage and shows them how to do it with empathy. Everyday Courage for School Leaders *is an outstanding read for anyone new to leadership and those who need to revitalize their thinking.*

Peter DeWitt, Author/Consultant
Corwin
Albany, NY

A great resource to support leaders as they revise priorities, reflect on their mission , and reassure staff, students, and community. Through their courageous leadership, we can accomplish our learning goals and achieve success.

Brenda Yoho, Director of Educational Support Programs
Danville District 118
Danville, IL

There has never been a time where we need more courage from educational leaders than right now. The ESSA provides new opportunities to rethink school improvement and accountability, but only the courageous need apply. Principals must be courageous lead learners willing to collaboratively inquire and develop themselves and their staff. This book tells you why and how to do this. It is a must read and a must do!

Brian A. McNulty, Partner
Creative Leadership Solutions
Lone Tree, CO

Dr. Lassiter has drawn upon her own experience as a principal, district administrator, and national educational consultant to write a book that is relevant to the immediate needs of school leaders. She clearly knows the many challenges, obstacles, stresses, and opportunities that school leaders face daily and provides clear guidelines for the development of courageous, effective leadership for anyone who wants to learn. Her work is grounded in research, best practices, her extensive experience, examples of courage from principals around the country, and includes a call to action for school leaders to take smart risks! This book should be on every superintendent's reading list for every principal, assistant principal, and district leader. It provides a guiding light to show the way to success and hope to all those school leaders who work so hard daily to improve the quality of teaching and learning for all.

Linda O'Konek, Consultant
Creative Leadership Solutions
Boston, MA

It is often said, "how goes the principal, goes the school." In Dr. Lassiter's second book, Everyday Courage for School Leaders, *the critical role of the school principal is the focus. With inspiring examples and deeply rooted research, Lassiter demonstrates the importance of everyday courage in leading a school.*

In interviews for school administration, one often must demonstrate skills such as decision making, communication, instructional knowledge, and organization. What goes unsaid is the critical need to be able to apply courage to the decisions, communication, and organization in the best interests of students. Lassiter reminds her readers that schools are for students, that courageous leaders often must make decisions about adults, and that their actions are not always popular or supported. Everyday courage cannot be learned in a degree program. It must be nurtured and developed through trust, accountability, and risk-taking. These "three Cups of Courage" empower leadership and form the basis of this encouraging and thoughtfully written book for school leaders.

Karen Branscombe Power, President
East Coast Education Leaders Inc.
New Brunswick, Canada

This material is comprehensive, extensive, focused, and practical. The personal anecdotes of real principals help to illustrate the essentials of the chapters' main themes. This book certainly makes a strong case in support of the importance of leadership courage. School leaders need this type of thinking now more than ever before and have little in the literature from which to draw. This book will fill that void.

Ainsley B. Rose, Author/Consultant
Corwin
Thousand Oaks, CA

Everyday Courage for School Leaders

For Brittany, Blake, and Tim

Everyday Courage for School Leaders

Cathy Lassiter

CORWIN

A SAGE Publishing Company

A SAGE Publishing Company

FOR INFORMATION:

Corwin

A SAGE Company

2455 Teller Road

Thousand Oaks, California 91320

(800) 233-9936

www.corwin.com

SAGE Publications Ltd.

1 Oliver's Yard

55 City Road

London EC1Y 1SP

United Kingdom

SAGE Publications India Pvt. Ltd.

B 1/I 1 Mohan Cooperative Industrial Area

Mathura Road, New Delhi 110 044

India

SAGE Publications Asia-Pacific Pte. Ltd.

3 Church Street

#10-04 Samsung Hub

Singapore 049483

Executive Editor: Arnis Burvikovs

Senior Associate Editor: Desirée A. Bartlett

Editorial Assistant: Kaitlyn Irwin

Production Editor: Bennie Clark Allen

Copy Editor: Lana Todorovic-Arndt

Typesetter: C&M Digitals (P) Ltd.

Proofreader: Eleni-Maria Georgiou

Indexer: Jean Casalegno

Cover Designer: Anupama Krishnan

Marketing Manager: Nicole Franks

Printed in the United States of America

ISBN: 978-1-4522-9125-3

This book is printed on acid-free paper.

SFI® Certified Sourcing
www.sfiprogram.org
SFI-00453

17 18 19 20 21 10 9 8 7 6 5 4 3 2 1

Contents

Preface

This book is a celebration of the 150,000 principals and countless other school administrators that lead our nation's schools. These men and women rise every morning knowing the day ahead will bring challenge, frustration, and exhaustion, but also inspiration, exhilaration, and satisfaction. It takes courage, determination, and stamina to succeed in the principalship, regardless of the kind of school you lead. I invite you to read, reflect, and enjoy this book that aims a spotlight on the leadership courage required of school leaders today. Not heroic courage, but the courage needed day in and day out to improve instruction, create a supportive school culture, build trust, take risks, and create schools that change children's lives.

I hope that this book spurs a national conversation about the courage it takes to lead America's schools today. Professional organizations representing school leaders understand and acknowledge that leaders cannot lead if they are fearful. Further, they understand that no school improvement agenda can be realized without the courageous leadership of the principal. So, it stands to reason that more attention should be given to leadership courage and more intentional support provided to principals to enable and empower their courageous leadership.

A UNIQUE PROPOSITION

This book stands out from other books on educational leadership in that it centers on the idea of courage as a necessary component of leadership. Unlike other books on the market, *Everyday Courage* offers a practical and engaging guide to help school leaders understand more deeply the role that courage plays in exceptional school leadership, while providing useful, easy-to-use tools to assess your current Courage Quotient and assistance for taking specific action to move toward more courageous leadership practices.

- **Guiding Principles.** The core of the book is based on three foundational ideas:

    1. *Leaders must have the courage to lead an agenda based on equity and excellence for **all** students.*

    2. *Courage is a learned trait and can be strengthened with the right mindset and practice.*

    3. *Strong instructional leadership requires everyday courage.*

- **Three Daily Practices.** Like your daily cup (or cups) of coffee, everyday courage is a daily practice, conceptualized here as consisting of trust practices, accountability practices, and risk-taking practices.

- **Principal Profiles.** To bring these practices to life, storytelling plays a significant role in the book. Each of the practices are illuminated by vignettes from courageous principals.

- **How to Take Action.** Rather than just reading about courage practices, readers will be asked to make specific plans and to take action on those plans. I offer specific, action-based practices critical for effective school leadership in each of the three Cups of Courage.

- **Courage Quotient.** Readers will engage in self-reflection and assessment about their own strengths and areas for growth. You will have a chance to assess and reflect on your use of everyday courage at the end of each chapter via the learning activities and then in a more comprehensive way with the assessment instrument in Chapter 7, where you can determine your Courage Quotient (CQ) score.

An Indelible Impact on Your Leadership Practice

As a result of engaging in this book, school leaders will develop a keen awareness of the daily courage required to perform the duties expected of them. You will have the opportunity to self-assess and reflect on your current professional practices. Reflective prompts will ask you to drill down into specific areas of action in each of the three categories of courageous leadership (trust, accountability, and risk-taking). The book will lead you through a winnowing process to determine two or three focus areas for deliberate practice, and assist you in developing a sound plan to build your capacity in your identified focus areas. You will be empowered as a school leader to take charge of building the courage it takes to lead well every day.

For online resources, please log on to **www.corwin.com/everydaycourage**.

Acknowledgments

First and foremost, this book is a celebration and recognition of the courageous principals who lead our schools. I am forever grateful to the 10 principals who so graciously shared their experiences to illustrate the many ways school principals activate their courage every day to effectively lead their schools. These 10 leaders spent hours with me in person, on the phone, or via email to share their successes and challenges in order to make the concept of everyday courage meaningful to readers. These leaders are:

Olivia Amador-Valerio
Finney Elementary School
San Diego Public Schools
San Diego, CA

April Brown
Main Street Elementary
   School
Chester Upland School District
Chester, PA

Ashton Clemmons
Brooks Global Magnet School
Guilford County Schools
Greensboro, NC

Stanley Law
Arlington Community Junior/
   Senior High School
Indianapolis Public Schools
Indianapolis, IN

Sarah Manzo
Oakview Middle School
Lake Orion Community Schools
Oakland, MI

Dawn Massey
Florosa Elementary School
Okaloosa County Schools
Fort Walton Beach, FL

Emily Paul (retired)
Good Shepherd of the Nativity
   School
Archdiocese of New Orleans
New Orleans, LA

David Sauer
Mineola High School
Mineola Independent School
   District
Mineola, TX

Tommy Thompson
New London High School
New London Public Schools
New London, CT

Walter Perez
Harry McKillop Elementary
Melissa Independent School District
Melissa, TX

I also offer sincere gratitude and acknowledgement to the senior leaders at Corwin who have created an organizational culture that fosters creativity, empowerment, and joy for the people who work there. Thanks to Mike Soules, President, and Lisa Shaw, Senior Vice President and Managing Director, who demonstrate a genuine interest in helping all people achieve their career goals. Thanks also to Kristin Anderson, Senior Director of Global Consulting and Evaluation, who believes in the greatness in all of us. She had the audacity to see it in me and is the reason I am a successful author and consultant. Without the encouragement and confidence from Kristin, and the supportive culture of Corwin, I would never have finished this book.

Additionally, I truly appreciate the support and guidance from the editorial team. Arnis Burvikovs kicked life back into this book after it lay dormant for some time. His knowledge and experience were invaluable throughout the process. I also appreciate Desirée Bartlett and Kaitlyn Irwin for their support and assistance along the way. Many thanks to the copy editors and marketing and sales teams for their interest and hard work in getting the book out to leaders in the field. I am so grateful to be part of the Corwin team—a team that strives daily to provide extraordinary professional services and publications to educators worldwide.

Finally, and most importantly, heartfelt thanks to my wonderful family and friends for their unconditional support and encouragement along the way.

Corwin gratefully acknowledges the contributions of the following reviewers:

Bruce Clemmer, Director ELL
  Division
Clark County School District
Las Vegas, NV

Linda O'Konek,
  Consultant, EdD
Creative Leadership Solutions
Boston, MA

Brian A. McNulty, Partner, PhD
Creative Leadership Solutions
Lone Tree, CO

Ainsley B. Rose
Author and Consultant
British Columbia, Canada

About the Author

 **Cathy Lassiter** is an international consultant with over 30 years of combined experience as a public school teacher, principal, central office administrator, and consultant. Cathy is an author consultant for Corwin Learning, and she is a certified consultant for Deep Equity developed by Gary Howard, and Visible Learning for Literacy developed by Douglas Fisher, Nancy Frey, and John Hattie. Cathy consults with districts and schools in the areas of instructional leadership, school culture, change management, curriculum, and assessment. She is the author of *The Secrets and Simple Truths of High-Performing School Cultures,* published in 2012, and she has coauthored numerous books, including *Activate: A Leader's Guide to People, Practices and Processes*, as well as *Getting Ready for the Common Core State Standards* handbook series. She has also served as an adjunct professor for The George Washington University, teaching graduate courses in educational leadership.

As a successful middle school principal, she concentrated on meeting the needs of all students by imposing rigorous standards and high expectations. She was named Virginia's Middle School Principal of the Year for the success of her school. As a nationally recognized teacher, Cathy proved her ability to successfully reach students from all backgrounds. Her passion continues to be working with leaders and teachers to change the lives of all students by improving the education they receive each and every day.

Cathy lives in Virginia and Florida with her husband, Tim, and has two children, Brittany and Blake.

Introduction

Courage is more exhilarating than fear, and in the long run it is easier. We do not have to become heroes overnight. Just a step at a time, meeting each thing that comes up, seeing it is not as dreadful as it appeared, discovering we have the strength to stare it down.

—Eleanor Roosevelt

COMPLEX TIMES

School leadership is not for the meek or the weak, nor is it for sensitive souls. It is tough, demanding, and frustrating work, and it takes courage every day to do the job well. Courageous leaders are in high demand in schools today resulting from the significant increases in expectations driven by politicians and business leaders unsatisfied with the performance of public schools. These changes have led to fear-based school and district cultures, creating unprecedented levels of anxiety and job dissatisfaction. According to a study conducted by MetLife in 2012, workplace stress in schools is at the highest levels in decades, driven in large part by fear. In these situations, people tend to keep their heads down and keep to themselves, attempting to fly under the radar in order to survive. This not only applies to teachers, but to leaders as well.

These are the times that call for bold, determined, confident, courageous leadership. As history has shown, those with the guts to step forward take some personal and professional risks to lead change during times of uncertainty and establishing the new normal.

THE GUIDING PRINCIPLES

The guiding principles at the core of the book center squarely on providing schools for children and their families that enrich their lives and position them for opportunities to thrive, excel, and fully realize their life's potential.

Guiding Principle 1

Leaders must have the courage to lead an agenda based on equity and excellence for *all* students.

As outlined in the 2015 *Professional Standards for Educational Leaders,* effective leaders adopt a social justice agenda to provide an empowering education for all students. An agenda of equity and excellence must serve as a leader's guiding light and a beacon on the hill when making tough decisions.

This requires a culturally responsive school culture where all adults work in service of all students. It requires that all adults embrace an equity-based mission and vision and deliver instructional excellence to every child, every day. It is the principal's responsibility to establish this kind of school culture and promote a vision, mission, and core values in service of what is right and just for all students. This work requires the kind of courage in focus in this book.

Guiding Principle 2

Courage is a learned trait and can be strengthened with the right mindset and practice.

The second guiding principle of the book is that courage can be learned. Many people think of courage as a natural personality trait or born talent, but emerging research in psychology and neuroscience shows that courage can be learned and practiced. In short, human beings are not born courageous or cowardly: These are learned behaviors (Nili, Goldberg, Weizman, & Dudai, 2010; Rachman, 1983; Worline, Wrzesniewski, & Rafaeli, 2002).

Guiding Principle 3

Strong instructional leadership requires everyday courage.

The third guiding principle is the importance of strong instructional leadership from the principal. According to research by McKinsey and Company, "the only way to improve outcomes [in schools] is to improve instruction" (Mourshed, Chinezi, & Barber, 2010).

Based on this research, as well as numerous other studies on the power of instructional leadership, it is clear that effectively leading instruction and being known as a credible instructional leader among staff is the most important role of school administrators today. It takes courage to not only learn about what works best in our classrooms, but also to measure and respond to the impact instruction has on student learning. The development of everyday courage empowers and facilitates strong instructional leadership, thus making a discussion on courage both timely and necessary.

How the Book Is Organized

PART I: CHAPTERS 1 AND 2

Part I on the book establishes the *what* and the *why* of everyday courage for school leaders. In Chapter 1, I endeavor to create a common language about courage for school leaders, by clearly defining what is meant by *everyday courage*. Everyday courage for school leaders includes moral courage, intellectual courage, disciplined courage, and empathetic courage. Each of these types of courage are discussed in detail.

In Chapter 2, I make the case for why a discussion on courage is essential to school leaders today. We are losing our leaders at alarming rates for a myriad of reasons, all of which can be linked to courage. Additionally, any discussion on courage also requires some attention to fear. Overcoming fear is the key to leading courageously, and it will also be examined in Chapter 2.

PART II: CHAPTERS 3–5

Part II of the book takes the discussion from defining and understanding everyday courage to practicing everyday courage. In Chapters 3–5, the practices of everyday courage are examined in detail. Because everyday courage is needed like a daily cup of coffee, the specific practices of everyday courage are organized into three Cups of Courage. Each cup of everyday courage contains the practices or drops of courage that are essential for courageous leaders, and each of the practices are illuminated by stories from principals from around the country in the Principal Profiles.

The three Cups of Courage include

Trust Practices

Chapter 3

Accountability Practices

Chapter 4

Risk-Taking Practices

Chapter 5

In Chapter 3, the first Cup of Courage on trust is discussed. Trust is foundational to everything that is accomplished or not accomplished in a school. When organizational trust is lacking, suspicion, doubt, and fear take over, and people become miserable, unhappy, unhealthy, and uncommitted to the work. Trust can be built by implementing a few but powerful practices, even during times of uncertainty. These will be discussed in Chapter 3.

In Chapter 4, the discussion moves from trust practices to accountability practices. Courageous leaders build accountable cultures. Personal accountability from the leader first, followed by the staff, creates tremendous opportunities for growth, renewal, and positive collective action.

Collective accountability, internal accountability, and reciprocal accountability are also factors in building an accountable culture in schools, and all will be addressed in Chapter 4.

Finally, in Chapter 5, the third Cup of Courage (risk-taking) is presented. Leaders who engage in courageous leadership every day understand that risk-taking is part of the job. Leading with core values of equity, excellence, and inclusion, and embracing innovation and design thinking, are risks worth taking. Fearlessly focusing on what matters most and modeling resiliency in the face of inevitable setbacks are practices that enable risk-taking, all of which are discussed in this chapter.

Finally, Part II focuses on specific courageous practices that exemplify moral, intellectual, disciplined, and empathetic courage. These practices, or Cups of Courage in the areas of trust, accountability, and risk-taking embody the essence of courageous leadership, and they provide information about the specific actions that enable a person to lead courageously.

PRINCIPALS TO LEARN FROM

Throughout Parts I and II, you will find real stories from practicing principals that illustrate leading from a courage mindset. The featured leaders were selected from the many principals I have worked with over the years as a consultant, and some I have worked with for 2 to 3 years. Others were selected based on my knowledge of their work and/or recommendations from superintendents and trusted colleagues. They were not selected based on test scores or awards, although some of them have outstanding results and have earned national recognition. They were selected based on their courage to lead and do the hard work of school improvement every day. I have seen unbelievable courage in leaders whose schools are labeled as "low performing." They are making great progress in improving instruction, transforming school culture, embracing personal accountability, and taking risks to move the needle on achievement.

These principals represent a wide range of schools. They range from National Blue Ribbon schools to former high school drop-out factories. They are large and small, urban, suburban and rural, public and parochial. They have been recognized as America's Best High Schools and Title I Most Improved Schools, but they have also been federal turnaround schools and improvement-required schools. These schools are located across the country from San Diego to the French Quarter in New Orleans to the inner city of Indianapolis to the Emerald Coast in Florida. These leaders represent you. The everyday hard working principal striving to provide a world-class education to all students. I was inspired by each of them and in awe of the leadership courage they demonstrate on a daily basis. I think you will find rich learning opportunities in their stories.

PART III: CHAPTERS 6 AND 7

Part III of the book emphasizes personal activation of everyday courage by moving from information to application and activation. You will engage in self-reflection and learn about deliberate practice planning to strengthen your courageous leadership.

Chapter 6 specifically applies the findings from psychology and neuroscience, to help you develop a courageous mindset and build strength for courageous action. Self-reflection and purposeful practice are the key ingredients to developing everyday courage in school leadership, and both will be discussed in this chapter.

In Chapter 7, you have an opportunity to validate the courageous practices you use now and learn about practices that will strengthen your leadership via the self-assessment and Courage Quotient (CQ) score. In addition to the CQ score, you will receive a Courage Profile in each of the three Cups of Courage: trust practices, accountability practices, and risk-taking practices. This profile will help you zero in on a few specific practices for growth, as well as strategy starters for your practice plan.

FINAL THOUGHTS

In Final Thoughts, everyday courage is revisited and summarized. The three Cups of Courage and the essential practices or drops are reviewed and synthesized, and final thoughts on how to use them for personal development are offered.

Finally, each chapter ends with a chapter summary to emphasize the main points in the chapter and learning activities for you to deepen your knowledge and apply your learning. I encourage you to review the summaries and try the activities before moving on to the next chapter.

PART I

Foundations for Everyday Courage

What Is Everyday Courage?

The courage of life is often a less dramatic spectacle than the courage of a final moment, but it is no less than a magnificent mixture of triumph and tragedy. People do what they must—in spite of personal consequences, in spite of obstacles and dangers and pressures—and that is the basis of all human morality.

—John F. Kennedy

THE EVOLUTION OF COURAGE

Early Greek philosophers, Plato, Aristotle, and Socrates, participated in spirited debates about the definition of courage. They were in agreement that courage was one of four virtues. The four virtues are prudence, justice, temperance, and courage. Aristotle is credited with saying that courage is the first of all virtues. It makes all other virtues possible. It was Socrates who asked, "What is courage?" He spent many hours with his students attempting to discover the answer to this question.

Plato's ideas about courage, found throughout his writings, liken courage to a kind of perseverance. He took into account and considered how courage related to everyday common activities such as facing sickness, poverty, pains, and fears. Aristotle's definition of courage was focused on physical courage, the courage of soldiers on the battlefield or the courage of men in defense of their families, and the role they play in keeping the *polis,* or city, safe. Aristotle's conception of courage was that courage as well as the other virtues represented a system of means between extremes. With courage, the two extremes were cowardice and rashness. A coward runs away in the face of danger, as opposed to the extreme of rashness, which is when a person faces danger in a careless or foolish manner. Courage is the mean between the two. After the many debates and discussions however, Socrates and Plato lamented that they never arrived at a definitive answer to the question, "What is courage?"

Throughout the centuries, ancient and modern peoples have attempted to define and understand courage. Philosophers, soldiers, and common citizens alike have struggled to understand what it is about an action that makes it courageous (Brafford, 2003, p. 1). Although the definitions of courage and courageous acts have evolved over thousands of years, some ideals have remained true—people want to be considered courageous, and courage is highly valued by nations. All around the globe, nations recognize and bestow honor upon those who are thought to have performed courageously. In the United States, honors for courage include the Medal of Honor, which is the highest honor given to recognize valor in American armed forces, the Profiles in Courage Award, which recognizes displays of courage described in *Profiles in Courage* by John F. Kennedy, and the Civil Courage Award, which is a human rights award given by the Trustees of The Train Foundation for steadfast resistance to evil at great personal risk. In Sweden, the Edelstam Prize is given to persons for exceptional courage in standing up for one's beliefs in the defense of human rights.

In modern America, beloved poet, novelist, and civil rights activist Maya Angelou reiterated the thinking of the early philosophers in many of her poems, stories, speeches, and interviews. She said,

> I am convinced that courage is the most important of all the virtues. Because without courage, you cannot practice any other virtue consistently. You can be kind for a while; you can be generous for a while; you can be just for a while, or merciful for a while, even loving for a while. But it is only with courage that you can be persistently and insistently kind and generous and fair. (Beard, 2013)

Upon Angelou's death in 2014, *Washington Post* writer Jena McGregor concluded,

> The world lost a great author, poet and civil rights activist Wednesday when Maya Angelou died at her home in Winston-Salem, N.C. It also lost someone who was a great student of leadership and the creative process—who understood what it takes to have the courage to lead, who had close affiliations with some of the most well-known world leaders of her lifetime, and who could articulate the virtues of courage, steadfastness and truth as only a poet can do.

Angelou wanted to be known as a courageous person, and as she passed at the age of 86, she was lauded for her many accomplishments, most notably her courage.

MODERN SCIENCE STUDIES COURAGE

Courage continues to intrigue human beings in the 21st century, over 2,000 years after Plato and Socrates failed to gain consensus on courage and courageous behavior. According to a collection of research studies on courage published by the American Psychological Association, titled *The Psychology of Courage: Modern Research on an Ancient Virtue* (Pury & Lopez, 2010), there is growing interest in courage and the quest to answer the question, "What is courage?" The study of courage is gaining momentum in the fields of psychology and neuroscience with over half of the research to date being done from 2000 to the present. The ultimate goal of the researchers, however, extends far beyond the early philosophers' question and broadens to the following questions:

> Why does courage matter?
>
> Can courage be learned?
>
> Can courage be leveraged to improve organizational performance?
>
> As part of the research chronicled in this text, a synthesis of the many descriptions and definitions of courage proposed in the fields of philosophy, social sciences, literature and lexicons, was provided. (Pury & Lopez, 2010, pp. 52–53)

After extensive consideration of the descriptions and definitions, I am choosing to use the definition offered by Rate, Clark, Lindsay, and Sternberg (as quoted in Pury & Lopez, 2010) to define everyday courage for school leaders. When I speak of everyday courage throughout the book, it will be defined as (a) willful, intentional act; (b) executed after mindful deliberation; (c) involving objective substantial risk to the actor; (d) primarily motivated to bring about a noble good or worthy purpose; (e) despite, perhaps, the presence of the emotion of fear. In essence, courageous actions include risk, fear, purpose, and deliberate action, all of which are relatable and necessary in the day-to-day challenges of school leadership.

> Everyday courage is (a) willful, intentional act; (b) executed after mindful deliberation; (c) involving objective substantial risk to the actor; (d) primarily motivated to bring about a noble good or worthy purpose; (e) despite, perhaps, the presence of the emotion of fear.

Further, contemporary thinking about courage encompasses all areas of modern life and contains the notion that there are many different kinds of courage, much like Plato's early thinking on the subject. According to Steven Kotler (2011), author, journalist, and writer for *Psychology Today*, there are many types of courage in modern society. In his blog, "Courage: Working Our Way to Bravery: A Modern Examination of the Real Requirements of Fortitude," he describes physical courage, battle courage, moral courage, intellectual courage, empathetic courage, emotional courage, fiscal courage, stamina, and decision making.

Everyday Courage for School Leaders Defined

In relationship to the everyday courage needed for school leaders, I am borrowing from Kotler's moral courage, intellectual courage, and empathetic courage, and adding disciplined courage to provide a description of everyday courage relevant to school leaders. Figure 1.1 provides an illustration of the four domains of everyday courage for school leaders as well as thumbnail definitions of each of the four domains of everyday courage.

FIGURE 1.1 Domains of Everyday Courage

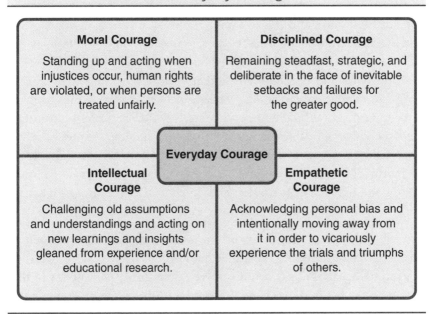

Moral Courage

Standing up and acting when injustices occur, human rights are violated, or when persons are treated unfairly.

Disciplined Courage

Remaining steadfast, strategic, and deliberate in the face of inevitable setbacks and failures for the greater good.

Everyday Courage

Intellectual Courage

Challenging old assumptions and understandings and acting on new learnings and insights gleaned from experience and/or educational research.

Empathetic Courage

Acknowledging personal bias and intentionally moving away from it in order to vicariously experience the trials and triumphs of others.

In the following sections, the domains of everyday courage are discussed in greater detail to clarify and explain each one as it relates to the work of school leaders. I have included an illustrative example in each section in the principal profiles. These profiles convey the stories and experiences of principals like you who demonstrate everyday courage.

MORAL COURAGE

Moral courage is the courage to stand up for one's beliefs in the face of overwhelming opposition. It is a synonym for civil courage. Those with moral courage stand up and speak out when injustices occur, human rights are violated, or when persons are treated unfairly. Moral courage is the outward expression of the leader's personal values and core beliefs, and the resulting actions are focused on a greater good. According to the research, what distinguishes moral courage is brave behavior accompanied by anger or indignation, which intends to enforce society or ethical norms without consideration for one's own negative consequences (Greitemeyer, Osswald, Fischer, Kastenmueller, & Frey, 2006). It is best exemplified by the actions of people such as Mahatma Gandhi, Nelson Mandela, or Rosa Parks.

As it relates to moral courage for school leaders, Leithwood, Harris, and Hopkins (2008, p. 28) point out that principals can have an impact on pupil learning through a positive influence on staff beliefs, values, motivation, skills, and knowledge, and ensuring good working conditions in the school, and that these factors all contribute to improved staff performance. They further report that in recent studies in the United States and United Kingdom, what stood out among the leaders who undertook the challenge of taking on very difficult-to-serve schools was their "'moral purpose,' a fundamental set of values centered on putting children first and faith in what children can achieve and what teachers can do." The moral purpose of improving the lives of children is ever-present and directs the leaders' actions and decisions toward that end. In short, moral courage for school leaders acts in service to all students.

For school leaders, it might involve intervening in and changing school practices that overidentify African-American male students for inclusion in special education, or it could involve maintaining persistence in dismissing a teacher who has been doing educational harm to students and previous leaders have failed to act and failed to spare students a wasted year in their learning. Moral courage compels action that ensures the social, emotional, and academic well-being of all students. Finally, moral courage is inclusive of several other types of courage and as such is an essential component of everyday courage in school leadership.

The Principal Profile that follows provides a rich example of moral courage from Tommy Thompson of Connecticut.

Principal Profile

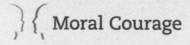 **Moral Courage**

Tommy Thompson

New London, Connecticut

When Tommy Thompson became the principal at New London High School in New London, Connecticut, he observed many practices that challenged his moral compass. New London serves 977 students, where

80% are students of color and 70% are economically disadvantaged. There was an entrenched faculty that operated on a "this-too-shall-pass" mentality and an unspoken agreement of "you leave us alone and we will leave you alone." Students were not graduating prepared for the rigors of college and careers, and they were not being challenged academically in their classes. The school ran as a factory model with all students receiving the same instruction regardless of their needs or entry level knowledge and skills. During our interview, Tommy stated, "Free agency among teachers abounded." As the father of four sons, he knew this was not something he could accept. He felt, and continues to feel, a moral obligation to the parents of his students, and committed to do all he could to transform the culture of the school to embrace a students-first, equity-based mindset.

Tommy understood that if things were going to change, it meant that he had to be the change agent on behalf of the students, and he also knew that change agents don't last long in the job. He stated to me during our interview, "you have to do a gut check and be able to look yourself in the mirror and say, 'if this means I will only be here a short time then so be it.'" He could not accept the status quo, knowing that students were at risk of not graduating, not achieving, and not reaching their life's fullest potential.

Tommy went to work putting structures and routines in place that included the use of common formative assessments, weekly PLC meetings, and follow through on expectations for quality instruction every day. He made sure his expectations for teaching and learning were clearly communicated to the staff, and he worked hard to provide support, resources, and guidance to help teachers make the required shifts. He worked cooperatively with the teacher union to assist teachers on assistance plans. High expectations resulted in some teachers choosing to leave the profession, while he recommended nonrenewal of contracts for others who would not or could not improve their teaching practices to satisfactory levels.

As a result, the union representatives were frequent visitors to the school. Tommy learned a lot through these exchanges, and he came to

(Continued)

(Continued)

know the teacher contact inside and out. He learned to work within the language of the contract to provide teachers due process and assistance. Tommy stated that he disagrees with people who say it is impossible to remove ineffective teachers due to teacher unions. He found that it is quite possible, but you have to be willing to do the work. Teachers should be afforded every opportunity to improve, but in the end, if they are harming students and are unwilling to improve, or the learning curve appears to be too steep for the individual, then the principal must do whatever is needed to remove them. Tommy has demonstrated the wherewithal to see his expectations though to the end on behalf of student learning. Tommy stated to me, "to do anything else would be educational malpractice."

After 8 years, Tommy's moral courage is paying off. In 2015, New London High School was named one of U.S. News and World Reports Best High Schools for their work in closing achievement gaps and the performance of the students in various subgroups.

The next domain of everyday courage is intellectual courage.

INTELLECTUAL COURAGE

The second component of everyday courage for school leaders is intellectual courage. Intellectual courage is the courage to challenge old assumptions and understandings and act on new learnings, understandings, and insights gleaned from experience and/or educational research. Paul and Elder, thought leaders at The Foundation for Critical Thinking, a nonprofit organization dedicated to improving education worldwide through the cultivation of critical thinking, describe intellectual courage as being conscious of the need to face and fairly address ideas, beliefs, or viewpoints toward that we once opposed or have not given serious consideration (The Critical Thinking Community, n.d.).

Intellectual courage is relevant to school leaders because, inevitably, we will come to see value in some ideas not previously thought to be valid or important. We need the courage to recognize the limitations of our own thinking in such circumstances (Lombardo, 2011). New research evidence and advancements in the science of learning are reported regularly at conferences and in research journals. This contemporary research is sometimes contradictory to present-day practices and beliefs about what works in schools and classrooms. School leaders must be open to new findings, ideas, conclusions, and recommendations that have the potential to revolutionize their thinking. In the end, we must all be willing to say: "I used to think . . . Now I think . . . because of . . ."

Think of Galileo's courage to argue that the Earth revolves around the Sun based on scientific evidence, or Columbus' theory of sailing west to get to the east on a spherical world, or modern environmental scientists arguing that climate change and global warming are the result of man's toxic gas emissions and destruction of rain forests. This kind of courage likens to John Hattie's revolutionary research in *Visible Learning* (2009). Many old assumptions about what works *best* in education have been disproven, thus challenging educators, policy makers, and researchers to rethink positions on certain instructional practices, and thereby enlightening all to other instructional practices that new research shows works best for students. Hattie calls on educators to "know thy impact." For leaders, this means changing from a focus on teaching to a focus on learning. It means having the intellectual courage to look critically at the impact our actions and practices have on student learning and adjusting our actions accordingly to improve our impact on student learning.

Further, Hattie calls for educators at all levels to face and address the most stubborn of barriers to student achievement: the variability in learning from classroom to classroom within a school. Hattie believes appropriate attention to this problem has not come to bear because it requires uncomfortable examination of the quality of teaching and teachers in our schools (Hattie, 2015). Why is it that some teachers have a significant impact on students' learning and others have no impact at all? How can we learn from those who are positively impacting student achievement? And, how can we leverage that professional capital for the benefit of more students?

Finally, successful school leaders demonstrate intellectual courage when they seek to learn and understand contemporary research and share their thinking with the school community about current practices that either are or are not working for students. Failure to do so, or failure to act on what we know is best for students, is the opposite of intellectual courage, it is actually intellectual cowardice, and some might argue is morally unacceptable. Intellectual courage is a call to action to close the infamous knowing-doing gap. We know what works best in education, but it takes courage to act on this knowledge to lead change on behalf of all students.

In the following Principal Profile, Emily Paul provides a compelling example of how principals activate and leverage their intellectual courage to impact student learning.

Principal Profile

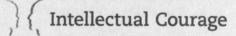 **Intellectual Courage**

Emily Paul

New Orleans, Louisiana

Emily Paul, principal of Good Shepherd School of the Nativity, provides us with an excellent example of leadership characterized by intellectual courage. Good Shepherd is a Catholic school located in New Orleans' French Quarter serving a student body that is 100% African-American and 100% economically disadvantaged. The students are in the "scholarship" program administered by the Archdiocese of New Orleans, which enables students from the public school system to attend the Catholic schools on scholarships paid for by the state of Louisiana.

Emily has been a principal for over 20 years at various Catholic schools with the last 7 years as principal at Good Shepherd. With well over 45 years in education, she has seen and learned a lot about what works for students. She has never lost her desire to learn and improve, and she has endeavored to stay current in educational research in order to support her teachers in using practices that research shows work best for students.

I have been witness to Emily's work as her instructional coach and as a professional developer for the Archdiocese for over 2 years. At each opportunity to learn new practices, Emily attended professional learning sessions with her teachers. She and her teachers focused on implementing high-effect-size practices including teacher collaboration in data teams, linking cause and effect data to build collective teacher efficacy, using a formative assessment process to encourage student ownership in learning, and creating lessons that build students' conceptual understanding. Emily consistently reinforced the teachers' efforts and followed through to ensure that they learned, improved, and helped each other refine these practices in all of their classrooms. Emily continues to demonstrate intellectual courage by acting on new research, following through to support her staff who are implementing new practices, and using data to measure the impact new practices are having on student learning.

Emily was equally vigilant about her own learning of the research and high-effect-size practices, and her intellectual courage has made a difference at Good Shepherd. State test results in 2015 ranked Good Shepherd number two among all schools in Louisiana for student performance. In 2016, after the first administration of the PARCC assessment, Good Shepherd ranked seventh among all schools for overall student performance. The school has received many recognitions and accolades from the Archdiocese and the Louisiana Department of Education.

The team at Good Shepherd is evidence driven, and they understand that their actions precede student learning outcomes. They intervene early, they adjust what they are doing, they use research-based strategies, and they learn from their mistakes. The infamous "knowing-doing gap" does not exist at Good Shepherd, and the students are the clear beneficiaries of the intellectual courage and wise leadership from Mrs. Paul.

Disciplined courage is the third domain of everyday courage. It is discussed in detail below.

Disciplined Courage

The third component of everyday courage is disciplined courage. Disciplined courage is the courage to be reflective, strategic, and focused in the face of constant distractions and opposition. It is what Aristotle called the mean between the extremes of cowardice and rashness. This kind of courage helps leaders focus on the greater good and is usually morally based. Leaders with this brand of courage have great clarity on their vision and the impact they want to have on those in the school community. They are focused on doing the right things, in a thoughtful and purposeful way. Mike Staver (2012), author of *Leadership Isn't for Cowards*, explains it this way, "Courage is about clarity and mindfulness—clarity about what you believe and mindfulness in the execution of those beliefs in the culture" (p. 14).

Disciplined courage enables leaders to steadfastly address important issues and maintain a focus on the goal or desired outcome. When setbacks and disappointments occur, disciplined courage helps leaders stay the course, connect with their resolve, and persevere through the challenges and keep moving. It also allows them to keep their emotions in check in order to learn from the opposition and compromise along the way in order to achieve the intended outcome with the integrity of the goal intact.

Disciplined courage is in direct opposition to blind courage. Blind courage is uncontrolled courage, and it could get you fired. It is oftentimes spontaneous, emotive, passionate, or rash, as Aristotle described. It is sometimes grounded in good intentions or righteous thinking, and may sometimes lead to positive changes, but can often result in unintended consequences. For example, school leaders who violate teacher contracts, even if it is for a good cause, as opposed to finding a way to the goal within the contract or working to change the contract, might be said to have blind courage. School leaders who exempt certain students from state testing because they believe the test is inappropriate for the students, as opposed to finding a solution within the testing guidelines, may also be said to have blind courage. Their cause may be noble, but their blind courage will not end well for them or their schools.

The Principal Profile that follows provides an example of the real challenges principals face today and a great story to learn from as you strive to activate your disciplined courage.

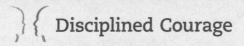 Disciplined Courage

Ashton Clemmons

Guilford County, North Carolina

Ashton Clemmons, principal of Brooks Global Magnet School in Guilford County, North Carolina demonstrates the kind of discipline and stick-to-itness that exemplifies disciplined courage in schools. Brooks serves students from all around the district who are chosen through a lottery system. Students do not have to meet any entrance criteria in order to go into the lottery draw. Therefore, the school serves a wide cross section of students including low-to-high socioeconomic status, as well as students of color representing various cultural backgrounds including African-American, Asian, and Latino families.

When Ashton arrived as the new principal at Brooks after spending 4 successful years in a very challenging Title I school, she was quite surprised at the practices in her new school. Known for their success, Brooks is one of the highest-performing schools in the district, lauded for their rigorous global studies curriculum. Ashton was expecting strong instructional pedagogies, progressive learning environments, and high expectations for all students. She was surprised to find this was not the case in all classrooms, and she was concerned about stark inconsistencies in the quality of instruction from classroom to classroom, and within classrooms as well. Although Brooks is high performing, significant achievement gaps existed among ethnic and socioeconomic groups.

To provide a quality learning experience for all students, Ashton communicated her core values to the staff in "Clemmons' Norms," which she brought with her from her previous school. These norms govern her leadership practices and how she works with students and staff. They are posted on the wall in her office. They include the following:

(Continued)

(Continued)

- It is our responsibility to spend all of our time focused on student learning.

- If what we are doing is not working for the child, then adults will change their practices.

- We all will continually improve and get better.

As Ashton attempted to lead in accordance with these norms, she experienced a number of challenges along the way. For example, teachers had become accustomed to sitting students in the hallways when they became disruptive or nonresponsive. When they weren't sitting in the halls, they were sent directly to the office. Not only was this practice in violation of the district's discipline process, but it was also contributing to the achievement gaps in performance. Students cannot learn if they are not in class. As Ashton insisted that the teachers follow the district's discipline referral process, a small group of vocal teachers and parents tried to derail the changes. Rather than express their concerns directly with her, they held secret meetings to criticize her leadership, and they created and circulated a petition for her removal, which was sent to her regional superintendent and school board representative. This led to a face-to-face meeting with the regional superintendent where the group expressed their displeasure with the way Ashton was running the school.

All the while, Ashton stayed focused on her core values and the purpose of her work. She stayed steady and calm, and strategically kept plugging away at improving instruction and implementing the district's discipline policy. She exemplified disciplined courage in very difficult circumstances. Her courage was grounded by clarity and mindfulness mentioned earlier in this chapter. Clarity about what she believes and mindfulness in the execution of those beliefs.

Ultimately, Ashton was supported by the school board and her supervisor, which reflects their commitment for equity and excellence in all of Guilford County's schools. Ashton attributes their support to her past work in the district and her success as a principal, as well as her courage to stand by her core beliefs that all students deserve the very best education.

Ashton has demonstrated disciplined courage by remaining true to her core beliefs and taking clear, strategic steps to create a school culture in which adults accept responsibility for the learning of all students, and to her, all means *all*.

The final domain of everyday courage is empathetic courage.

EMPATHETIC COURAGE

The final type of everyday courage is empathetic courage, or the courage to open up and feel deeply for others. Without this, the previous three types of courage become impotent. It takes humility and courage to put aside your own biases and assumptions and let go of control and certainty for the sake of learning something new. But it is only when you are willing to listen to a different perspective, and manage to empathize, that you can be enriched by a new way of thinking.

Daniel Goleman (2006), psychologist, author of 10 books, and two-time Pulitzer Prize nominee for his work on emotional intelligence, tells us that there are three kinds of empathy all leaders need to know and use. These three types of empathy include cognitive empathy, emotional empathy, and empathetic concern.

Cognitive empathy is the ability to see the world through another person's eyes. It helps us connect with another person's mind giving us a mental sense for how they think and see things. This is a critical skill in the workplace that enables strong relationships and effective communication to motivate, inform, and support the people we work with.

Emotional empathy allows us to tune into the feelings of another person and read their facial, vocal, and a stream of other nonverbal signs that illustrate how they feel. According to Daniel Siegel, a UCLA psychiatrist, connecting with people on this level creates a "we" chemistry in the brain that builds rapport and understanding that results in productive and meaningful work for both parties.

The third type of empathy is empathic concern, or expressing care and concern about another person. Leaders accomplish this kind of connection when they show people that they will be supported and that they can trust the leader. This encourages people to take risks, try new approaches, and open up to others for collaboration and team learning. Goleman stresses that it is essential for leaders and teachers to have all three kinds of empathy.

Empathetic courage also means acknowledging our biases up front and intentionally moving away from them. You have to effectively parse these thoughts out from yourself. This frees you to start vicariously experiencing the trials, tribulations, and triumphs of others, and muster the courage and conviction to decide to go where they are.

Examples of empathetic courage, which includes Goleman's three types of empathy, might include holding students and staff to high expectations while empathizing with them as they struggle with learning something new and experiencing failures along the way. Or, holding a student accountable for unacceptable conduct while also showing empathy for the student's challenging home life. A leader demonstrating empathetic courage might insist on implementing new reading or math programs, while seeking to understand and experience the challenges teachers are having along the way, in order to help them through the change process.

In the end, the reward is worth the risk. The reward is a genuine understanding of the human condition that helps you earn trust, gain respect, build teams, and engage all stakeholders in work for the greater good.

Following the tragic death of 46-year-old Beau Biden from brain cancer in May, 2015, his father, Vice President Joseph Biden made an appearance on *The Late Show With Stephen Colbert*. During the interview, he said this about his son, "He had so much courage; he had so much empathy." He was equally proud that his son was both courageous and empathetic. It is a powerful combination of traits. If a person is both courageous and empathetic, it would seem that he is willing to take wise risks, while having strong feelings of concern and even love for others (Lieber, 2015).

The Principal Profile that follows features Dawn Massey from Florida. Her leadership philosophy provides an informative example to learn from when it comes to leading with empathy in your school.

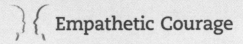 Empathetic Courage

Dawn Massey

Okaloosa County, Florida

Dawn Massey, principal of Florosa Elementary School in Okaloosa County Schools in Florida, is a leader who demonstrates courage and empathy. She leads through a servant leadership mindset and believes her role as principal as one who sets high expectations, while genuinely caring for the people on her team.

During our interview, Dawn explained that when she began her principalship, she reflected back on a leader from her past who had a significant positive influence on her development as an educator. She thought about the leadership style and specific practices of this leader and asked herself, what did he do that motivated me to achieve challenging goals, trust in his leadership, and give 110% effort each day? She wanted to be a leader who could connect with people at this level and inspire them to achieve great things. She concluded that this leader trusted his staff to make the right decisions for students, and he empowered them with shared decision making to run the school with him.

Dawn inherited a school characterized by low trust, suspicion, hidden agendas, and fear. Florosa is a Title I school serving a large percentage of economically disadvantaged students. Their school rating from the state of Florida was a grade of C when Dawn took the helm. She knew they were capable of much more, but she had to build trust and develop strong relationships with the staff before she could push them to heights they were capable of achieving. Dawn expressed her genuine concern for the teachers at Florosa and her desire to empower them to run the school, just as her previous leader had done. She firmly believed that, by building trust, creating a caring culture, and empowering the staff through shared decision making, student achievement

(Continued)

would soar. She was right. Florosa went from a C school to an A+ school in just 2 years. Dawn gives full credit for their success to her staff. Her role in the success of the school is as lead collaborator with the team.

Finally, Dawn considers herself a member of the team whose major contribution is recognizing and leveraging the talent of her people to serve the needs of all students. It is important to her that every day teachers have joy while working hard in service to students. She exclaimed, "Joy and rigor is what it is all about!"

Dawn's courage to see the school through the eyes of the teachers, her ability to tune in to their feelings and fears, and her genuine concern for their well-being makes her an excellent example of a school leader with empathetic courage.

Finally, everyday courage, including moral, intellectual, disciplined, and empathetic courage, requires explicit practice and discipline. It is tempered, thoughtful, planned, and moderated. It is morally based and works in service of all students. It is intellectually grounded, while maintaining a strong connection to the human condition. Everyday courage promotes and facilitates leadership from the whole person—the heart, the head, and the gut. It calls for leaders to be in touch with the courage that lies within them and to use that courage to keep unproductive fear at bay. School leaders need to skillfully leverage all four types of everyday courage to succeed in their complicated roles. In the next section, you will learn about courage and the brain, and how you can control your thoughts to develop a courage mindset.

THE NEUROSCIENCE OF COURAGE AND FEAR

In addition to the growing body of psychological research on courage, neuroscientists are beginning to explore how courage operates in the brain. While much research is available on fear in the brain, research specifically on courage is more limited, even though the two are closely linked. Just as the researchers listed earlier wanted to expand the scope of understanding courage, so too do the brain researchers. Their questions about courage include the early philosophers' quest to answer, "What is courage?" as well as the psychologists' questions previously discussed, which include:

Why does courage matter?

Can courage be learned?

Can courage be leveraged to improve organizational performance?

Neuroscientists are expanding the scope of the research and seeking answers to the questions below:

Can we train our brain to act courageously?

Can brain stimulation activate courageous behavior?

Can medications modify or enhance courage activity in the brain to treat anxiety and stress disorders?

Uri Nili and colleagues (2010) at the Weizmann Institute in Rehovot, Israel, designed a study to measure fear and document courage by monitoring brain activity during a fearful event using MRI scanning. About 60 people volunteered for the study, and they were separated into two groups. One group, the Fear Group, was composed of 40 people who were found to have a serious, debilitating fear of snakes. This group was determined by a questionnaire that graded their fear level toward the live snakes. The other group, the No Fear Group, was composed of 20 people who handled snakes on a regular basis and had absolutely no fear of the animals.

In Part 1 of the study, subjects laid in an MRI machine and saw either a live snake or a teddy bear at the end of a conveyor belt located near their heads. They were asked to choose either "Advance" or "Retreat" options on a button, and when the choice was selected, the snake or teddy bear moved closer or farther away from them. No one in either group was afraid of the teddy bear. But, in the No Fear Group, there was no difference in selection of advance for either choice, live snake or teddy bear. To them, the snake was as safe as the stuffed animal.

In Part 2 of the study, the participants were instructed to bring each object as close as possible to their heads, even if they were experiencing significant fear. Of course, no fear was involved with the teddy bears, and some subjects were able to bring the live snake closer, but a larger percent of this group chose "Retreat" to move the snake away. After each button selection, the participants were asked to report their fear level on a scale of 0–100. Those in the Fear Group reported, on average, a 62 score of fearing the snake. In addition to the after-selection question, the participants were also monitored with a brain scan and an SCR, or skin conductance response that measures sweating when nervous. The after-selection questions helped to determine how much courage the participants summoned in order to bring the snake a step closer. The Fear Group participants recognized their mounting fears, and some were able to force themselves to overcome their fear and press the button to bring the snake closer.

The researchers discovered that a courage center in the brain lit up when the Fear Group showed courage by moving the live snake closer despite their fear. This part of the brain is the sgACC, or subgenual anterior cingulate cortex, which is responsible for fear, emotion, stress, perception, and a variety of other tasks. The powerful thing about this is that when you show courage and face your fear, the courage center or sgACC is activated, and when you succumb to your fear, it is not.

Interestingly, as the sgACC activity increased, the sweat-related skin conductance response decreased. Also, other MRI monitored regions of the brain were quieted by the courageous act, namely the amygdala. The amygdala is connected to the sgACC and helps to generate the body's arousal when certain kinds of emotion, such as fear, are triggered. The researchers believe that the sgACC helps the brain to overcome fear and dampens the fear-related arousal response. This research indicates that when the sgACC is activated by a courageous act, it is actually able to cancel out some of the fear response activated by the amygdala. "Fear is fundamental to survival," says study coauthor Uri Nili. "But the human brain makes us capable of overriding it to a certain point. When there's a strong motivation, the sgACC sends out orders to inhibit the amygdala's fear response" (Nili, Goldberg, Weizman, & Dudai, 2010).

The researchers reported their findings in the June 2010 issue of *Neuron* (a research journal for neuroscience). It is the first study to show that activity in this area of the brain is needed for a person to act despite a natural fear. Mauricio Delgado, a neuroscientist at Rutgers University in New Jersey noted that from the MRI data, the researchers found that the increased activity of only one brain region, the sgACC, correlated with high fear levels, advancing the live snake, suggests that this region was involved in the successful mastery of fear. The conclusion is that courage trumps fear in the brain.

Why should school leaders care about this? Given the perpetually demanding work in schools, and the constant string of crises to solve, the brain may get stuck in fear overdrive. This is what leads to stress and anxiety. Knowing how the brain works up the courage to confront fear could help. With this knowledge, perhaps we can learn to activate courage to trump fear when dealing with difficult situations. In the meantime, the lesson from this research is that to overcome fear and practice everyday courage, we have to purposely engage in acts of courage. These intentional acts will provide the necessary exercise of our brains to build the muscle needed for continued courageous acts.

> According to neuroscience, courage trumps fear in the brain.

CONCLUSION

I began this chapter with a brief overview of the evolution of courage in societies. Courage has been considered a virtue for thousands of years, and still today that remains true. Since 2000, however, the scientific community, psychologists and neuroscientists, have become intrigued with the concept of courage that they have launched numerous studies which might explain courageous behavior or pinpoint how it works in the human brain. For school leaders, I provided a working definition of everyday courage that was born from the work in the scientific community and then further explained everyday courage by providing a description of the four types of courage relevant to the daily work of school principals.

In the next chapter, I will further make the case for the focus on everyday courage and provide a rationale for a national conversation on the topic.

Chapter Summary

Key Points

- Courage has been a valued virtue by people for thousands of years.

- Modern researchers define courage as (1) a willing, intentional act; (2) involving substantial danger, difficulty, or risk to the actor; (3) primarily motivated to bring about a noble good or morally worthy purpose.

- Everyday courage for school leaders involves the appropriate use of four domains of courage including

  1. Moral courage

  2. Intellectual courage

  3. Disciplined courage

  4. Empathetic courage

- Neuroscientists have discovered a courage center in the brain that is activated when a person behaves courageously. When this center comes on, fear responses decrease.

- In order for school leaders to develop everyday courage, they must intentionally ignite the courage center in their brains. They do this by facing their fears head on and doing more of what they fear most.

- School leaders must activate all four types of everyday courage to eliminate fear and establish a high-performance culture in their schools.

Chapter 1

Learning Activity: Reflect and Assess

The purpose of this activity is to reconnect you with examples from your past when you were courageous in an effort to learn from these previous acts of courage and replicate them with current difficult situations. The four domains of everyday courage are listed below. Choose one or more where you have demonstrated courage in the past and respond to the questions that were derived from the modern definition of courage. Record your answers in the spaces provided. Make note of how you might tap into past acts of courage with current challenges knowing that courage is developed by acting courageously over and over.

Moral Courage		
Standing up and acting when injustices occur, human rights are violated or when persons are treated unfairly.		
What actions did you take?	What difficulties or risks did you face?	What noble good or moral purpose was achieved?
What challenge(s) are you facing now where moral courage is needed?		
What will you do, based on your previous success above, to address your current challenge(s)?		

Intellectual Courage		
Challenging old assumptions and understandings and acting on new learnings, and insights gleaned from experience and/or educational research.		
What actions did you take?	What difficulties or risks did you face?	What noble good or moral purpose was achieved?

What challenge(s) are you facing now where intellectual courage is needed?

What will you do, based on your previous success above, to address your current challenge(s)?

Disciplined Courage		
Remaining steadfast, strategic, and deliberate in the face of inevitable setbacks and failures for the greater good.		
What actions did you take?	**What difficulties or risks did you face?**	**What noble good or moral purpose was achieved?**

What challenge(s) are you facing now where disciplined courage is needed?

What will you do, based on your previous success above, to address your current challenge(s)?

Empathetic Courage		
Acknowledging personal biases and intentionally moving away from them in order to vicariously experience the trials and triumphs of others.		
What actions did you take?	**What difficulties or risks did you face?**	**What noble good or moral purpose was achieved?**

What challenge(s) are you facing now where empathetic courage is needed?

What will you do, based on your previous success above, to address your current challenge(s)?

Making the Case for Everyday Courage

> *You may encounter many defeats, but you must not be defeated. In fact, it may be necessary to encounter the defeats, so you can know who you are, what you can rise from, how you can still come out of it.*

> —Maya Angelou

THE UNSPOKEN REQUIREMENT

There is no question that the job of leading schools is harder now than ever. States across the nation have revised, or are in the process of revising, their leader evaluation systems to include multiple measures and greater accountability for student achievement outcomes. The public expects schools to educate their children on much more than academics including how to be safe online, appropriate use of social media, safe sex, the dangers of bullying, avoiding drugs, and how to be safe in an active-shooter situation. Students arrive at school with social, emotional, and academic needs that must be attended to in order for them to learn. Central office leadership demands for compliance on any number of issues exacerbate principals' frustrations and add to the complexity of the job, and teachers need and deserve quality professional development and coaching to help all students learn at high levels.

What is missing from the current narrative about effective school leadership, in light of all of the challenges, is an acknowledgment and discussion about the courage it takes to lead a school. It is surprising that the issue of courage is absent from conversations about school leadership, and it does not have a prominent place in state-level leadership standards or principal evaluation systems, nor is courage an essential characteristic in the newly adopted national standards for educational leaders. However, I believe anyone reading this book would agree that a school leader cannot be successful or effective without everyday courage. It is the most essential unspoken requirement of the job.

In the next section, I will share the requirements in the new national standards for educational leaders. These standards provide a good backdrop for why everyday courage is a necessity in developing great leaders for our schools.

Professional Standards for Educational Leaders

In October 2015, the National Policy Board for Educational Administration (NPBEA) released new standards for school and central office leaders. The Professional Standards for Educational Leaders 2015 (PSEL 2015) replaces the Interstate School Leaders Licensure Consortium (ISLLC) standards that have shaped the landscape of educational leadership for the last 20 years. These new standards represent the best thinking of a wide array of stakeholders including the National Association of Secondary School Principals (NASSP), National Association of Elementary School Principals (NAESP), American Association of School Administrators (AASA), as well as highly regarded thought leaders in the field, university professors, research organizations, and school leadership practitioners, including superintendents and principals.

They are to be commended for their work, as the standards are the most forward-thinking, rigorous, research-based standards to date, providing states, districts, and universities clear guidance and direction for leadership development, performance evaluation, and professional learning opportunities. The standards clearly convey a keen national interest in inclusion, equity, excellence, and cultural responsiveness. Their collective thinking is spot on given the changing demographics of our school systems and our nation at large. According to the document,

> The 2015 Standards embody a research- and practice-based understanding of the relationship between educational leadership and student learning. Improving student learning takes a holistic view of leadership. In all realms of their work, educational leaders must focus on how they are promoting the learning, achievement, development, and well-being of each student. The 2015 PSEL reflect interdependent domains, qualities and values of leadership work that research and practice suggest are integral to student success. (Professional Standards for Education Leaders, 2015, p. 3)

PROFESSIONAL STANDARDS FOR EDUCATIONAL LEADERS 2015	
Standard 1. Mission, Vision, and Core Values	**Standard 6. Professional Capacity of School Personnel**
Effective educational leaders develop, advocate, and enact a shared mission, vision, and core values of high quality education and academic success and well-being of each student.	Effective educational leaders develop the professional capacity and practice of school personnel to promote each student's academic success and well-being.
Standard 2. Ethics and Professional Norms	**Standard 7. Professional Community for Teachers and Staff**
Effective educational leaders act ethically and according to professional norms to promote each student's academic success and well-being.	Effective educational leaders foster a professional community of teachers and other professional staff to promote each student's academic success and well-being.
Standard 3. Equity and Cultural Responsiveness	**Standard 8. Meaningful Engagement of Families and Community**
Effective educational leaders strive for equity of educational opportunity and culturally responsive practices to promote each student's academic success and well-being.	Effective educational leaders engage families and the community in meaningful, reciprocal, and mutually beneficial ways to promote each student's academic success and well-being.

(Continued)

PROFESSIONAL STANDARDS FOR EDUCATIONAL LEADERS 2015	
Standard 4. Curriculum, Instruction, and Assessment Effective educational leaders develop and support intellectually rigorous and coherent systems of curriculum, instruction, and assessment to promote each student's academic success and well-being.	**Standard 9. Operations and Management** Effective educational leaders manage school operations and resources to promote each student's academic success and well-being.
Standard 5. Community of Care and Support for Students Effective educational leaders cultivate an inclusive, caring, and supportive school community that promotes the academic success and well-being of each student.	**Standard 10. School Improvement** Effective educational leaders act as agents of continuous improvement to promote each student's academic success and well-being.

Source: NPBEA, 2015.

These standards signify a tall order for school leaders. They include over 80 elements that provide elaboration on the work necessary for proficiency. It is within these elements that the high expectations for school leaders become clear and specific. For example, Standard 1 focuses on mission, vision, and core values. It contains seven elements. *One* of those elements is provided below to illustrate the depth and breadth of the expectations for school administrators. Effective school leaders

> articulate, advocate, and cultivate core values that define the school's culture and stress the imperative of child-centered educa-tion; high expectations and student support; equity, inclusiveness, and social justice; openness, caring, and trust; and continuous improvement. (p. 9)

Additionally, in Standard 2 on ethics and professional norms, *two* of six elements are provided here to further convey the demands and require-ments of modern school leaders. Effective leaders

> Safeguard and promote the values of democracy, individual freedom and responsibility, equity, social justice, community, and diversity. . . .

Provide moral direction for the school and promote ethical and professional behavior among faculty and staff. (p. 10)

Finally, in Standard 3 on equity and cultural responsiveness, *one* example of the eight elements indicates that effective leaders

Confront and alter institutional biases of student marginalization, deficit-based schooling, and low expectations associated with race, class, culture and language, gender and sexual orientation, and disability or special status. (p. 11)

I share these examples not to be critical, but to build a case for why we need to focus on courageous leadership in schools. I wholeheartedly support these standards based on over 20 years of combined leadership experience as an assistant principal, principal, and central office administrator, as well as 10 years as a consultant working with leaders across the country. These 10 standards and the 80 plus elements *are* the best practices for school leadership, as difficult and complex as they might be. Some are more complex and demanding than others for sure.

After reading just these four examples, it should be very clear that a quality discussion about courageous leadership is necessary. Leaders are expected to cultivate and advocate for the core values of equity and social justice, confront, and alter institutional bias, and provide moral direction to staff and students. Additionally, effective leaders lead instructional practice that is rigorous, authentic to students and is differentiated and personalized (Professional Standards for Education Leaders, 2015, p. 12). Proficient leaders, according to the standards, develop teachers' professional knowledge using adult learning theory, and they deliver actionable feedback for improvement using valid, research-based systems of evaluation (p. 14).

Finally, in Standard 10 on school improvement, in Element 82, courage is mentioned as an expectation. It states that effective leaders

Manage uncertainty, risk, competing initiatives, and politics of change with courage and perseverance, providing support and encouragement, and openly communicating the need for, process for, and outcomes of improvement efforts. (p. 18)

If you take a closer look at this element, you will find that school leaders are expected to "manage" uncertainty, risk, competing initiatives, and politics. As a former adjunct professor teaching courses in educational leadership to prospective administrators, I do not recall seeing course material related to teaching people how to manage these complex issues, and these skills are not something they would have developed in the classroom as teachers. Furthermore, I do not know if it is possible to actually teach people to manage uncertainty, risk, and politics without including support for the development of their courage and provide the tools to facilitate determination and perseverance toward that end. These standards cry out for a leader's intentional activation and application of moral, intellectual, disciplined, and empathetic courage as described previously.

Districts must include courage as an essential component of their professional development of leaders. The consequences of not making courage part of the agenda for leadership development and not setting new leaders up for success will be long lasting. They will be addressed in the next section.

LOSING OUR LEADERS

American schools are on the verge of a leadership crisis. We are losing our most valuable school improvement resource—highly effective school principals. In a survey conducted by MetLife in 2012 and reported in February 2013 titled, *The MetLife Survey of the American Teacher: Challenges of School Leadership* (Markow, Macia, & Lee, 2013), 75% of school principals reported their responsibilities have "changed significantly in recent years, leading to a job that principals say has become too complex and highly stressful" (p. 1). Principals' job satisfaction is declining and is at the lowest point in over a decade. Teachers' job satisfaction has dropped to the lowest levels in 25 years. Nearly half of the principals surveyed feel under great stress several days a week.

Interestingly, in the face of increasing challenges, stress, and declining control over important decisions, nearly 89% (Markow et al., 2013) of principals agree that they should be held accountable for everything that happens to their students while at school. Clearly, accepting accountability for the children in their care is not at issue, as some critics may want the public to believe. Principals strive every day to meet the diverse needs of all of their students, and they do so because they believe it is their responsibility.

That being the fact, the MetLife study also showed that approximately one-third (32%) of current principals are likely to leave the profession for another occupation. If this statistic is applied to the entire principal body in the United States, it amounts to a loss of nearly 50,000 principals. These leaders were highly successful teachers and teacher leaders who earned advanced degrees and stepped up the take on the challenges of leading a school. It would be a travesty for our nation's schools to lose these leaders.

Additionally, very few candidates are lined up to take these jobs based on the survey data, which show that 69% of teacher leaders, specifically those who serve as department chairs, grade level chairs, coaches, mentors, or leadership team members, are not at all interested in becoming principals (p. 5). Couple this with baby boomer retirements and we will find that we are in a leadership crisis beyond any in the history of American public schooling. It is clear that the demand for quality leaders is growing, and the pool of qualified candidates is shrinking, which subsequently means that efforts to recruit and prepare qualified leaders must be accelerated. This must include a discussion on leadership courage and overcoming fear to lead successfully.

Future plans for grooming successful school leaders in these challenging times has to include the intentional development of everyday courage as described in Chapter 1. It is the antecedent to effective instructional leadership, progressive human capital management, and outstanding organizational performance. Leaders who are able to intentionally activate their courage when necessary will reap the benefits of increased confidence, empowerment, enjoyment, and efficacy about their work. As importantly, when leaders demonstrate moral, intellectual, disciplined, and empathetic courage they will enjoy greater staff support and engagement, high collective teacher efficacy and a culture of high performance. Developing everyday courage is worth the effort and the exigencies of the job call for it.

> When leaders demonstrate moral, intellectual, disciplined, and empathetic courage, they will enjoy greater staff support and engagement, high collective teacher efficacy, and a culture of high performance.

In the next section, I will discuss the impacts of everyday courage and fear-based leadership.

OVERCOMING FEAR

According to Debbie Ford (2012), author of *Courage: Overcoming Your Fears and Igniting Self-Confidence*, paralyzing fears, repressed self-confidence, and untapped courage are the obstacles that prevent us from making powerful choices that are in concert with our best interests and deepest desires. We all have inner voices speaking to us about what decision to make, what direction to take, and what actions are best. Which voice we listen to is a matter of choice. School leaders must make the conscious choice to listen to the inner of voice of strength, confidence, power, and passion, as opposed to falling victim to the voice of fear, helplessness, and powerlessness. All too often, we make the mistake of thinking we cannot take bold action because we are not smart enough, or respected enough, or powerful enough. We may fear that we are inept, unworthy, or undeserving in some way. These fears are normal, but they prevent us from developing our courage and force us into a fearful existence. The only way to get past these fears is to acknowledge them and understand the very real power they have in keeping us from achieving our goals.

Leading from a fear-based stance is deadly to organizational performance and literally diminishes good health due to the stress and anxiety that comes with it, not only for the leader, but the followers as well. Fear causes frenzy-based decision making, which leads to confusion and uncertainty for people in the organization. Fearful leaders have fearful followers making it impossible for anything of significance or importance to get accomplished. Fear causes leaders to play it safe. Margie Warrell calls it "playing small" (Warrell, 2009). Playing it small means you avoid the risk, the failure, and the criticism, but you also fail to accomplish anything new, meaningful, or significant.

> Fearful leaders have fearful followers making it impossible for anything of significance or importance to get accomplished.

Fear can take over your thoughts and actions without your knowledge or understanding that it is happening, or the crippling effect a fear mindset has on our lives. Every negative, self-doubting thought undermines our inner strength and power to conquer challenges. Fear will have you believe that retreating and playing it small will keep you safe, even when the opposite is true. It will have you believe you can't when you can, you're wrong when you are right, you're weak when you are strong. It will have you believe that the journey ahead is too long and too difficult, and the cost is too high, when in reality, you are right, you are strong, and you can make the long journey to success. You *can* lead from a courage mindset (Ford, 2012).

Developing your everyday courage requires that you claim and name your fears and make thoughtful decisions to break the pattern of fear-based behavior. You have to be on alert for the early warning signs that your body gives you when you are experiencing fear. These signs might include anxiousness, anger, tensing up, becoming red faced or flushed, tightness in the neck, stomachache, headache, racing heart, sweaty palms, and/or heavy breathing. Pay attention to these signs and take control with deliberate actions to quiet the fear responses. Roselle (2006), author of *Fearless Leadership: Conquering Your Fear and the Lies That Drive Them*, recommends that we engage in self-questioning to get things back into perspective. With the emission of the early warning signs, we should ask ourselves:

- What in this situation is causing me to feel irrational fear?

- Who am I afraid of disappointing? Being rejected by? Or getting hurt by?

- How big of a deal is this really?

- What is the worst that can happen here?

- Will this be important 5 years from now?

Just slowing down long enough to ask and answer these questions will help put you in touch with your fears and then put them in proper perspective. It will also help in activating the courage center of the brain, which in turn will calm the part of the brain emoting fear. I provide greater detail about how to do this in Chapter 6.

IMPACTING OUR PEOPLE

As we begin to examine how our own everyday courage might impact the people we work with, I think a good place to start is by reading and reflecting on the words of Marianne Williamson on our deepest fear. This inspiring quote is from her book, *A Return to Love: Reflections on the Principles of a Course in Miracles*, published in 1992. These words have been quoted in movies, books, and speeches by some of the world's most famous courageous leaders including Nelson Mandela. As you read the quote, think about your leadership. Do you lead from a fear mindset or courage stance? Do you play small or let your light shine?

> *And as we let our own light shine, we unconsciously give other people permission to do the same.*
>
> *As we are liberated from our own fear, our presence automatically liberates others.*
>
> From "Our Deepest Fear" by Marianne Williamson,
> *A Return to Love: Reflections on the Principles of a Course in Miracles*, pp. 190–191.

The last two lines of the quote are the essence of how courageous leadership will impact the people around you. Just as fearful leaders have fearful followers, courageous leaders have courageous followers. Workers do not trust cowardly leaders. Demonstrating your everyday courage will lift the entire school community to greater heights. Everyone gets better when the leader leads from a courage stance. This is not just supposition, it is supported by research!

THE IMPACT OF COURAGE AT WORK

Worline and colleagues (2002) analyzed responses from over 200 managers and employees who responded to the following four questions:

1. Have you ever seen courage at work? If yes, please tell a story about what happened.

2. What made the event or situation seem courageous to you?

3. How did you feel during the event or situation?

4. Did anything in your work change as a result of the event or situation you described?

They documented numerous instances in which individuals who witnessed courage in others had subsequent higher levels of self-efficacy, a sense of organizational ownership, and a willingness to be engaged in work. In short, seeing courage first-hand had an empowering effect on employees and made them want to work harder for their organization.

The researchers concluded that bearing witness to the leaders' courage as well as courage from coworkers will result in an emergent, collective phenomenon of organizational agency, thus making the exhibition of courage central to organizational success. These findings are consistent with the conclusions reported in studies involving soldiers, whistleblowers, Holocaust resistors, and terminally ill people (Worline, Wrzesniewski, & Rafaeli, 2002).

Courage is part of the texture of the modern-day workplace. Tight deadlines, difficult relationships, admitting mistakes, and accepting failures are the kind of challenges people face on a daily basis (Worline et al., 2002).

In schools, this translates to high-stakes work where the lives of children hang in the balance. Leaders and teachers face constant internal and external scrutiny, and must perform high-quality, complex work with an appropriate level of urgency and consistency. Courageous leadership builds courage in workers. Courageous activity transforms the quality of connections people have with one another by strengthening and validating their core beliefs and purpose-driven missions, and by activating greater engagement in their work and stronger connections to the organization as a whole.

> Courageous activity transforms the quality of connections people have with one another by strengthening and validating their core beliefs and purpose-driven missions.

CONCLUSION

In conclusion, school leadership takes grit and guts. But, the prevailing myth is that this is only true for leaders in urban schools, or poor schools, or rural schools. The fact is that it is true in *any* school in America today, including suburban schools, Catholic schools, charter schools, and private schools. The national principal associations, NASSP and NAESP, understand the complexities of school leadership and advocate strongly for school principals at the national policy level; however, the importance of leadership courage gets little *explicit* attention at the national level. This book aims to change that. There is indeed recognition that the job is complex, difficult, overwhelming, and anxiety-ridden, but that has not translated to acknowledgement and support to help principals build the courage they need to be successful.

Principals and aspiring principals deserve to have this topic come to the forefront of discussions related to professional development for leaders. An understanding of the different types of everyday courage discussed in Chapter 1, and the realization that courage can be developed and learned can make a difference in principal efficacy and job satisfaction. Additionally, it has the potential to renew their inspiration, improve their sense of empowerment, return their joy and passion for the work, and transform their perspective on what is possible.

Chapter Summary

Key Points

- The United States is facing a leadership crisis with thousands vowing to leave the profession and precious few in the wings interested in stepping up.

- The new Professional Standards for Educational Leaders is a mandate for courageous leadership. Success will not be achieved with cowardly, fear-based leadership.

- Districts must give greater attention to grooming and placing qualified leaders in their schools as well as increase their investments in supporting leaders' development so that they can succeed in the job.

- Courageous leadership is the antecedent to effective instructional leadership, progressive human capital management, and outstanding organizational performance.

- Research confirms that when workers are witness to courageous acts from their leaders and coworkers, it results in higher levels of self-efficacy and organizational ownership.

- Courage does not exist without fear.

- Leaders must avoid falling victim to an inner voice of fear, self-doubt, helplessness, and powerlessness and instead listen to the voice of strength, confidence, and power.

- Leading from a fear-based stance is deadly to organizational performance.

- Professional development for leaders must include an emphasis on courage development, as the exhibition of courage is central to organizational success.

Chapter 2

Learning Activity: Leading From a Courage Mindset

The purpose of this activity is to assess your leadership mindset regarding a current challenge, fear versus courage, to help you conquer it from a courage mindset.

First, identify a leadership challenge facing you now in which you are experiencing stress, anxiety, or worry. Respond to the reflective questions below. Upon completion, go back and review your answers. Lastly, pay great attention to your answers in the last section. Use these answers to create positive self-talk statements and self-encouragement for facing the challenge. This will help to activate your courage center and provide the strength and fortitude to lead from a courage mindset.

Your Leadership Challenge		
What in this situation is causing your fear?	Who are you afraid of disappointing or hurting?	What is the worst that can happen?

Describe the best-case outcome for this challenge. How do you define success?

What type of courage will this require? Circle all that apply.

Domains of Everyday Courage

Moral Courage	**Disciplined Courage**
Standing up and acting when injustices occur, human rights are violated, or when persons are treated unfairly.	Remaining steadfast, strategic, and deliberate in the face of inevitable setbacks and failures for the greater good.
Intellectual Courage	**Empathetic Courage**
Challenging old assumptions and understandings and acting on new learnings and insights gleaned from experience and/or educational research.	Acknowledging personal bias and intentionally moving away from it in order to vicariously experience the trials and triumphs of others.

Everyday Courage

What experiences, skills, and knowledge do you currently possess that might contribute to your success in this situation?

Experiences

Skills

Knowledge

What is your next step, and subsequent steps, to move you to your desired outcome?

First......

Next......

Next......

Finally......

As you engage in tackling this challenge, be sure to review this information often. You have identified the best possible outcome and thought about what success will look like in this situation. You have determined what is causing your fear, and you have identified the applicable domain(s) of courage this challenge requires. You have also identified the skills, knowledge, and experience you possess that you can leverage for success in this situation, and you have outlined the steps you will take. Now, in order to activate your courage, you must face the challenge head on. Listen to the voice of strength and confidence. Remember, the exhibition of courage is central to organizational success. To build courage, you must act courageously.

PART II

Practicing Everyday Courage

The Three Cups

In Part II, the discussion transitions from the foundational information, which defines everyday courage and fear and provides a rationale for why you need everyday courage, to specifically how you practice everyday courage. In Chapter 1, a contemporary definition of courage from researchers Rate, Clark, Lindsay, and Sternberg (as quoted in Pury & Lopez, 2010) was shared, which describes courage as

> (a) willful, intentional act; (b) executed after mindful deliberation; (c) involving objective substantial risk to the actor; (d) primarily motivated to bring about a noble good or worthy purpose; (e) despite, perhaps, the presence of the emotion of fear.

Everyday courage for school leaders involves the acts of facing and conquering inner fears. Acts of courage will be different for all of you, but what is in common is that you confront the fear head on, in spite of the risk, for a moral purpose or greater good. Everyday courage for school leaders includes moral courage, intellectual courage, disciplined courage, and empathetic courage. See Figure 1.1 from Chapter 1 that defines each below:

These domains of everyday courage often overlap and are interdependent in any given situation. As you read about the courageous practices that follow in Chapters 3, 4, and 5, reflect on the types of courage required to engage in these practices. You might ask yourself as you read, What type of courage does this practice call for? If I need growth in this practice, what type of courage will I need to activate?

Keep in mind that the courageous practices in Part II overlap and are also interdependent depending on the situation. I organized the courageous practices under three main clusters, or Cups of Courage. Cups of Courage include trust, accountability, and risk-taking. Each Cup of Courage

FIGURE 1.1   Domains of Everyday Courage (From Chapter 1)

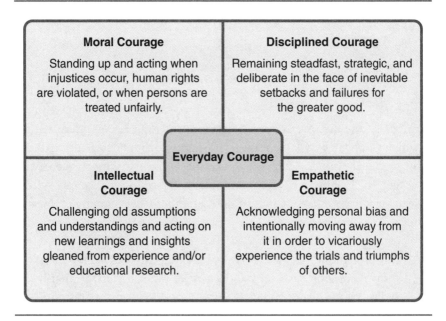

Moral Courage

Standing up and acting when injustices occur, human rights are violated, or when persons are treated unfairly.

Disciplined Courage

Remaining steadfast, strategic, and deliberate in the face of inevitable setbacks and failures for the greater good.

Everyday Courage

Intellectual Courage

Challenging old assumptions and understandings and acting on new learnings and insights gleaned from experience and/or educational research.

Empathetic Courage

Acknowledging personal bias and intentionally moving away from it in order to vicariously experience the trials and triumphs of others.

contains essential daily practices or "drops" for courageous leadership. Arguments could be made for putting some of the practices in a different cup or in more than one cup. But, they are placed and discussed in a manner to provide clarity and flow for understanding.

Figure P.II.1 illustrates how the domains of everyday courage—moral courage, intellectual courage, empathetic courage, and disciplined courage—relate to and provide a frame for the three clusters of courageous actions, or Cups of Courage, and the drops or specific practices of courageous leadership.

FIGURE PII.1   Framework for Everyday Courage for School Leaders

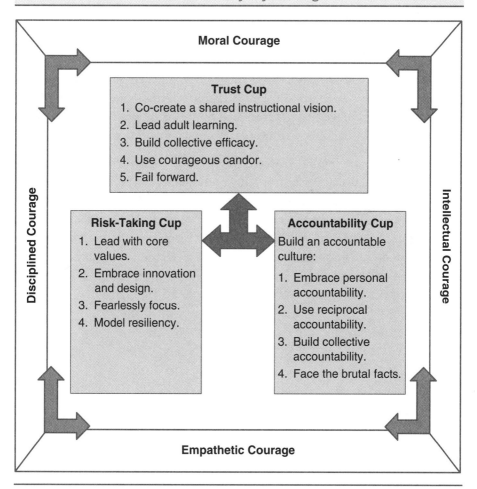

On the outside of the framework, there is a frame with each side representing one of each of the four domains of courage: moral courage, intellectual courage, empathetic courage, and disciplined courage. These four domains frame or anchor the specific practices of everyday courage on the inside of the frame. The arrows in the corners of the frame point in multiple directions to signify that they overlap. On the inside of the frame, there are three main clusters or Cups of Courage that include trust, accountability, and risk-taking. As illustrated, each Cup of Courage includes a list of courageous practices that will result in strong leadership in the three cups. Successful implementation of these practices rely on activating one or more of the courage domains on the outside frame of the graphic. The arrows connecting the three cups show that practices in trust, accountability, and risk-taking are not stand-alone silos, but rather that they are connected and interdependent. Each one is closely related to the other two.

Understanding how the domains interact with and frame the clusters or cups of courageous actions, and the specific practices in each cluster, will be essential to your work in Part III. You will assess the strength of your leadership courage in the three cups by specific practice, and determine next steps for building your everyday courage in areas where it is needed.

Finally, you are reminded that developing your courageous leadership is in service to becoming a strong instructional leader. Nothing changes for students unless the quality of the teaching they receive every day changes. In essence, the time and energy you spend in developing your everyday courage is an act of dedication to improving your instructional leadership and ensuring a quality teacher for every child, every day. The challenges of making this happen compels the implementation of the courageous practices that follow in Chapters 3 through 5.

☕ *Cup of Courage: Trust Practices*

> *Courage is what it takes to stand up and speak. Courage is also what it takes to sit down and listen.*
>
> —Winston Churchill

OVERVIEW OF TRUST

Courageous school leaders build trust, not by accident or happenstance, but intentionally and with purpose. Trust is the first Cup of Courage because trust is the foundation upon which everything else is built, and without it, courageous leadership is not possible. We all have our ideas about what trust is, but it is difficult to define because it is so complex. Textbook definitions generally indicate that trust is the belief that someone is good, honest, capable, or reliable. Megan Tschannen-Moran (2004), a researcher and professor at the College of William and Mary in Virginia, and author of *Trust Matters*, describes trust in schools as a glue and a lubricant. As a glue, trust binds organizational members to each other, and binds leaders to followers. As a lubricant, trust serves as a grease to organizational operations. It enables communication and cooperation among members. Without trust that is the glue that binds people together, and the grease that facilitates communication and cooperation, friction and heat are generated and can shut down organizational performance

(Tschannen-Moran, 2004). Trust is never already in place and is not possible without human effort. Trust cannot be mandated or directed. Deciding to trust is a choice. Trust in schools can be fostered and built by the actions of the leader, and it is a critical factor to their success.

Consequences of Distrust

Leaders who fail to cultivate a culture of trust between teachers and leaders and between and among teachers pay a heavy price. When trust is absent, people spend a lot of time in self-protection mode. They are constantly thinking about threats and hidden agendas. This is deadly to the currency in schools, which is student learning. Organizational energy is diverted from providing quality lessons to students to issues among the adults. Teachers become unwilling to take risks and will not extend themselves to their colleagues. Collegial sharing and collaboration in service of students is virtually nonexistent. Additionally, teachers will hold back information, suggestions, and their best ideas from each other and from the principal (Tschannen-Moran, 2004).

In a culture of distrust, administrators typically develop a variety of rules and compliance agendas to force people into the kind of teamwork and sharing they know makes a difference in student learning. But trust cannot be forced, and this effort is fruitless and counterproductive (Grover, 1992). Oftentimes, administrators will come to rely on control mechanisms to get people to do the things they should be intrinsically motivated to do. They will rely on directives, mandates, and monitoring, which do more to destroy trust than build it.

In this type of culture where command and control is the norm, teachers feel distrusted and micromanaged. They resent being treated as if they cannot be trusted to do their work well, and they start to hold back and do just enough to get by, and sometimes seek transfers to other schools. Micromanagement is the byproduct of distrust, and it is a morale killer. This is not to say that structures and routines should not be implemented and that people should not be held accountable. In fact, they should be. The norms of school life in a high-trust school include explicit expectations that people will be trusted to do their work and that members will assume positive intent of their colleagues. Strong teacher morale is linked to collegial trust and is necessary to create a high performing organization.

The most difficult challenge for leaders when distrust takes hold is that it grows and spreads, and it is difficult to build back. When organizational trust is lacking, suspicion, doubt, and fear take over, and people become miserable, unhappy, unhealthy, and uncommitted to the work. Not much of value can be accomplished if people are feeling this way! People do not believe that there are good intentions behind what others say and do, and there is a complete breakdown in genuine communication. The leader, too, is not seen as credible, which makes it extremely difficult to build trust back.

> When organizational trust is lacking, suspicion, doubt, and fear take over and people become miserable, unhappy, unhealthy, and uncommitted to the work.

In the next section, the focus is on the benefits of a culture of trust.

BENEFITS OF ORGANIZATIONAL TRUST

Leaders who successfully build and sustain organizational trust reap important benefits. Teachers in schools with high trust conduct their work from commitment to the vision and goals of the school rather than from compliance with orders and directives. They go beyond the call of duty and feel tightly bonded to their colleagues. There is strong internal accountability, and they do not want to disappoint their peers. Tschannen-Moran calls this "organizational citizenship," and these organizational citizenship behaviors are vital for productivity in schools. Only trust in and among organizational members can spur organizational citizenship.

Trust is also a lever for the development of collective teacher efficacy. Collective teacher efficacy is the extent to which a faculty as a whole believes they make a difference in students' learning. When teachers trust each other, they can focus on the work of improving teaching and learning as opposed to worrying about hidden agendas and unseen threats. Teachers and schools are much more likely to persist toward their goals if they genuinely believe they can accomplish them as a team. When a high level of trust prevails in a school, a sense of collective efficacy tends to be evident as well (Tschannen-Moran, 2004, p. 129).

"To be a trustworthy school leader takes courage" (Tschannen-Moran, 2004, p. 84). It also takes a leader willing to look in the mirror and accept

> When teachers trust each other, they can focus on the work of improving teaching and learning as opposed to worrying about hidden agendas and unseen threats.

accountability for the culture in a school. Trust must be built intentionally and without reservation because it is the foundation for what will be accomplished in the classroom by teachers and students. Leaders determine the culture in a school. Therefore, to have high organizational trust levels, your behavior must build and sustain trust for the good of the school community. Teachers need to trust you in order to cope with new expectations, new evaluations, new standards, and new accountability systems. They are being asked to change the way they work with colleagues and the way they deliver instruction to students. This is risky for them. Without trust, they will not push themselves to new ways of working with each other and with students, which makes it very difficult to accomplish challenging goals.

In the next section, I discuss the specific leadership practices that will help you build a culture of trust in your school. These are the practices or drops of courage, that fill the trust cup.

 ## LEADERSHIP PRACTICES THAT FILL THE TRUST CUP

Trust is the first Cup of Courage, for without trust the other courageous practices will not make a difference in school culture or in student achievement. These leadership practices are not the only ones that build trust, but they are significant contributors to high trust in schools. You are reminded that all of the practices in each of the three Cups of Courage overlap. There will be practices in Chapters 4 and 5 that can contribute to developing trust, but are also practices that are essential to the other two Cups of Courage; accountability and risk-taking.

Courageous leadership practices that build and sustain trust and fill the trust cup include co-creating a shared instructional vision and goals, leading adult learning, building collective teacher efficacy, using courageous candor, and failing forward by handling mistakes and missteps well. All of these practices are reflective of what the research tells us about building trust. These specific, research-based leadership practices are offered to help you discern the extent to which you use them, and the extent to which you build trust in your school.

CO-CREATE A SHARED
INSTRUCTIONAL VISION AND GOALS

Teachers across the country are confused and frustrated concerning how they are to conduct business in their classrooms. New evaluation systems have been implemented that contain as many as 60 indicators for success. Every state in the country has adopted new, more rigorous academic standards and along with them have come new textbooks, programs, and support materials. New professional development programs are being offered and each one has its own spin and favored set of best practices. It is no wonder that teachers are feeling cynical, overwhelmed, and burned out.

During times of complex change like these, teachers need a voice of reason, a voice that makes things simple, clear and doable. That voice must be yours. As mentioned earlier, teachers need to trust their leaders in order to push themselves to tackle the challenges they face today.

One way to gain their trust is to collaborate and work in partnership with them to sort out the expectations, clarify the changes, and create a clear instructional vision for your school. In the absence of such a vision, teachers will be left to figure it out for themselves and some will go the direction you hope and some will not. If you are to successfully lead *and* collaborate with teachers on the shared instructional vision, you must have a thorough knowledge of your state's academic standards, contemporary research on high-effect size strategies, teacher evaluation instruments, and district instructional expectations. With deep knowledge in these areas, you have the foundation to lead a collaborative effort with your teachers to create a shared vision of instructional excellence.

Teachers will have great insight and bring valuable contributions to the conversation, but as the instructional leader, it will be incumbent upon you to synthesize their thinking and clearly communicate the shared vision to all in your school community. This role cannot be delegated to other staff members. They can contribute, but you must lead.

Following the co-creation of the instructional vision, great clarity in messaging the vision and goals will be needed. You must be crystal clear about the instructional vision and goals. If teachers know the target, the instructional vision, and they know the instructional practices to use, they can self-assess and moderate their strategies and practices to move closer to the target. Feedback from leaders and coaches must be clear and move the teachers closer to the intended target or goal.

The Principal Profile that follows provides an informative look at one principal's approach to co-creating and communicating a shared vision of instructional excellence that you might use to get started in your school.

Principal Profile

}{ Creating a Shared Vision

David Sauer

Mineola, Texas

When David Sauer arrived at Mineola High School (MHS) in Mineola, Texas, he went right to work digging through the data from previous years to learn as much as he could about student achievement. When school opened, he spent the first semester going into classrooms to go beyond the numbers and observe the instructional program firsthand.

His analysis of the data and discussions with teachers revealed that students were graduating from Mineola High without the literacy skills they needed for college and careers. It did not sit well with him that students could not read or write on grade level and that the students were not literate for today's demands. He observed that they had low vocabulary skills, poor writing skills, and below-level reading skills; therefore literacy was at the top of his priority list.

Although he was apprehensive about sharing his assessment with a very established staff, he decided to give a State of the School address after the winter break. He opened the meeting by telling the staff that he was going to share his observations with them. He emphasized he was not blaming anyone or criticizing any one individual. He asked that they not speak or respond to the information, or ask questions. Rather, he wanted them to listen and reflect.

He was going to call them together to discuss the information in two weeks. His State of the School address included data on changing demographics over time, abysmal state test scores, and poor graduation rates. He shared specific academic results in the core contents as well. He emphasized the lack of a literacy program and the importance of literacy on the secondary level. He also provided some good news during his address. He recognized the positive climate among the teachers, and their willingness to work together to tackle significant challenges.

David also led the staff in a discussion about the school's vision and mission. He had done a lot of research on vision and mission statements prior to the meeting. He facilitated the meeting himself, based on what he had learned, to create the instructional vision for MHS in collaboration with the teachers. He divided the staff into work teams and took them through a process whereby they described a perfect school—one that students would want to attend and teachers would want to work. Each work team crafted a vision, and then the whole group synthesized all of the statements to create the MHS vision.

During our interview, David shared that the meeting ran late into the evening, but no one wanted to leave. They wanted to stay until it was done. He believes this meeting was the most important meeting of the year, as despite his apprehensions, the teachers became energized and excited about their future. Their shared vision would anchor their work going forward, as it provided clarity and direction about instruction with literacy at the core, it set expectations for student learning, and addressed the role of the school in the community. David took the lead in producing the final version using the teachers' input, and began using the shared vision immediately to guide all decisions.

This shared vision paved the path to success for MHS, that even David could not have foreseen. By leading from a courage stance, and activating his moral and intellectual courage, his work brought laudable improvements. Prior to his tenure, the English End of Course (EOC)

(Continued)

(Continued)

scores were below 60% passing rate. Two years later, after the implementation of the literacy initiative, the scores improved 20 percentage points and have been climbing each year since. Given that literacy is a focus in every academic class, other EOC test scores have dramatically improved as well. Algebra scores have increased from 67% to 90% in 4 years, and biology scores were 99% passing, the highest in the school's history. Through the use of uniform writing and note-taking formats that are used universally across the campus, the overall quality of writing has also improved dramatically.

In the next section, the importance of leading adult learning will be discussed as this is an essential component of realizing a shared instructional vision.

LEAD ADULT LEARNING

Once the instructional vision is clear, the next courageous practice necessary to fill the trust cup is leading adult learning. The research has clearly shown that the leadership practice having the greatest impact on student learning outcomes is the promotion of, participation in, and leading teacher learning and development (Robinson, 2011). Every bit of energy and effort exerted toward helping teachers learn pays dividends in student learning outcomes. Teachers thrive and learn in schools with a growth-oriented culture focused on adult learning.

Eleanor Drago-Severson, professor and researcher at Columbia University's Teacher's College, and author of numerous books, including *Leading Adult Learning* (2009), suggests that professional learning experiences for teachers should transition from solely informational to being transformational. Transformational learning's most basic principle is that adults experience learning, leadership, and their work-lives in qualitatively different ways and require differentiated supports and challenges to most effectively learn, grow, and care for students (Drago-Severson, 2004). Each teacher takes away a slightly or significantly different understanding from faculty meetings, speeches from the principal, and professional development sessions. The key is to lead for transformational learning, which helps teachers apply their understandings in ways that help the school and help improve student learning. Just learning new information in session after session will not transform classroom practice and will not help individuals effectively implement new programs and teaching strategies in their classrooms.

Make no doubt, there is a place for informational learning in schools. Some situations call for concrete, step-by-step instructive sessions to give teachers the nuts and bolts and how to's of a new program or instructional strategy. But this type of professional learning will not magically result in transformed practice in the classroom. In order for transformation to occur, teachers need both formal and informal opportunities to discuss implementation successes and failures and share lessons learned to help each other become more adept with a new approach. Integrating a new practice requires discussion, feedback from colleagues and coaches, classroom learning experiments, and collaborative work. These experiences help expose and circulate strong content knowledge as well as practical knowledge, good judgment, expertise, and accumulated wisdom in schools that is often confined to the classroom of the teacher who possesses that knowledge, wisdom, and expertise (Drago-Severson, 2004). To become better places for adults to learn and transform instructional delivery in classrooms, schools must intentionally become places where educators learn with and from one another.

Fullan and Hargraeves (2013) suggest that the way for principals to improve professional learning for teachers is to work with them in teams or groups. The current evaluation systems used by most districts require that leaders work with and coach teachers for improvement one teacher at a time. This is the most ineffective and inefficient way to spur growth and collective learning. If teachers are to transform their practice in the classroom, they need to have sessions with their colleagues, facilitated by coaches or instructional leaders to hear how the staff is progressing on new strategies; what they are doing well and what they need to continue to improve. Collective learning with peers is much more powerful than individual conferences with the principal.

It is up to the principal to ensure that the school is a learning organization, and that teachers learn with and from the principal. The profile which follows provides an example of how one successful principal leads adult learning.

} { Leading Adult Learning

Sarah Manzo

Lake Orion, Michigan

Sarah Manzo is the principal of Oakview Middle School in Lake Orion, Michigan, a suburban district 45 minutes outside of Detroit, Michigan. Lake Orion School District is a small district serving approximately 7,500 students. Oakview Middle serves 550 students with about 50 coming from the neighboring districts of Pontiac and Waterford, resulting from the district's school-of-choice program. Sarah is in her second year as principal at the middle school after spending 10 years as an elementary principal where she and her staff were awarded a Michigan Blue Ribbon for their outstanding work.

The district introduced standards-based grading several years ago. They implemented a phase-in plan starting with Grades K through 3. At the onset, Sarah emerged as a leader in learning about standards-based grading and then leading the learning of her teachers at the elementary level. She did research, attended conferences, and called in experts to deepen her own as well as her teachers' knowledge about standards-based grading.

Sarah focused her attention to leading the deeper learning and application of standards-based grading in her school. She organized weekly meetings with the teachers and focused each meeting on a key piece of the work. They tackled one issue at a time down to the greatest detail. She relied on the teachers as experts along the way, as they were invaluable to creating a standards-based system that would work well for students, parents, and teachers. Sarah served as a facilitator of the process and the learning. She trusted her teachers and supported them through their collaborations and shared decision making.

Leading adult learning on standards-based grading at the middle school has been a new challenge for Sarah, but she continues to emphasize that she is not the expert. She stresses she is learning with the teachers and looks forward to the continued collaboration with them to co-create a plan for standards-based grading in 2017. Sarah is building trust along the way, as teachers have a voice that is valued. They also have a leader who sees her role as lead learner with the staff.

In the next section, the focus is on building collective teacher efficacy as a powerful lever in building trust.

 BUILD COLLECTIVE TEACHER EFFICACY

As mentioned earlier in this chapter, collective teacher efficacy is the extent to which teachers believe that when they work together and collaborate around improving student learning, they make a significant difference in student learning outcomes. Collective teacher efficacy grows from collegial trust, and trust is strengthened when collective efficacy is built. Each one serves as fuel for the other. One way to determine the level of collective efficacy in your school is to attend teacher team meetings. Teachers' collective efficacy becomes very evident in team meetings and/or whole staff meetings when they discuss their current achievement data and challenges ahead. Consider the two scenarios that follow. One is indicative of a strong sense of collective teacher efficacy and the other is not. As you read each scenario, decide which one best represents teacher conversations in your school.

Scenario 1

Teachers in this fifth-grade PLC meeting are discussing the data from their most recent formative assessment on drawing inferences in literary text. Each teacher's data are projected on the screen, and they begin their analysis. Mrs. Smith notices that students were able to draw surface level inferences by using the graphic organizer the teachers had provided as part of the assessment. Mrs. Jones notes that things went downhill when the students were asked to draw inferences

(Continued)

(Continued)

that required students to connect information from the first paragraph of the text to the sixth paragraph and then use their background knowledge to determine the inference. And finally, Mr. Potts observes that students had difficulty with the vocabulary in the text and he provided examples of words that students struggled with. Following their analysis, the teachers began their collaboration on what to do next. They all acknowledged that drawing inferences in complex literary text is tough for fifth graders and that this group of students has struggled with it since the third grade, and possibly since kindergarten. They felt that their graphic organizer was a good tool to help students learn to draw simple inferences, and they agreed they would continue to use it with some modifications to help with more complex inferences. They also acknowledged that vocabulary was a barrier so they decided to add the use of the Frayer Model for teaching vocabulary in this unit, and they decided exactly how they would incorporate the model into their lessons. Next, they discussed helping the students keep track of their reading in longer passages by using a process for annotating the text as they read. Finally, the team talked about which of their new strategies would be used for all students in whole group instruction, and which ones would be used in small group instruction for specific students. They agreed to start instruction the next day and also agreed on the quick assessment they would give at the end of the following week to see if their strategies were having the intended impact on student learning. They also agreed to keep in touch on how things are going during their lunch and other times together.

Scenario 2

Teachers on this seventh-grade English Language Arts team gathered for their weekly meeting to discuss student progress on their standards. Each of the five teachers had given a common pre-assessment on drawing inferences from multiple pieces of literary text. They used a common scoring guide for consistency in determining proficiency. The results were provided in a spreadsheet that contained each teacher's results. Right away, members of the team noticed that the majority of students scored in the lowest performance band. They acknowledged that the assessment was rigorous and that the text was appropriately complex for the seventh grade. A sense of discouragement and frustration became evident as they talked about the challenges ahead for the team. Mrs. Olds lamented that every year, the elementary school sends students ill-prepared for the rigors of middle school. Her colleagues agreed and asked how could they be expected to close obvious gaps created in the elementary school. Mr. Young noted that the students were able to respond to the comprehension questions that preceded the questions requiring students to draw inferences. Mr. Bright added that he felt the students got lucky on those questions because his students could not read grade-level text that well. As the team moved the conversation to instruction each teacher shared what they planned to do in their classrooms. The strategies included think alouds to demonstrate how inferencing is done, worksheet practice with shorter pieces of text, and using sixth- and possibly fifth-grade text to give the students text they could comprehend in order to learn how to draw simple inferences first, and then more complex inferences as they progress. There was no discussion about using common strategies as a team. At the end of the meeting, they agreed they would reconvene in 3 weeks when the district benchmark test had been given.

When collective teacher efficacy is high, as indicated in Scenario 1, teachers trust in the abilities of their colleagues and themselves, and they exert a collective determination to roll up their sleeves and find what will work for each of their students. They openly recognize that they have challenges ahead, but they work together to move the students forward knowing that they can make a positive impact on student learning. They are empowered to solve their own problems, and they find strength in working with their grade level peers, as was illustrated in Scenario 1.

The teachers in Scenario 2 had solid practices in place; preassessments with grade level rigor and common scoring guides for all teachers. They had scheduled time for data analysis, and collaboration. But, their beliefs and expectations were not highly efficacious. They did not demonstrate a genuine belief that together they could improve students' learning, and they did not agree on instructional best practices that all students would benefit from. Finally, they failed to recognize the strengths that students demonstrated in comprehension of grade level text, which could have served as a bridge for building their inferencing skills. Instead, they contradicted their data and called the students lucky.

The research shows that the fifth-grade team in Scenario 1 will enjoy greater success than the seventh-grade team in Scenario 2. Bandura (1993) found that the effect of perceived collective efficacy on student achievement was stronger than the link between socio-economic status and student achievement. Additionally, John Hattie ranks collective teacher efficacy as the number one factor amongst all of the influences that impact student achievement, and Eells' meta-analysis demonstrates that collective efficacy and student achievement are strongly related with an effect size of 1.57 (Donohoo, 2016).

Principals who focus on building trust have a much greater chance of generating collective teacher efficacy in their schools. Without trust, teachers tend to work as independent contractors and not team members. In the profile which follows, principal Dawn Massey shows how she built collective teacher efficacy at her school.

Principal Profile

 **Building Collective Teacher Efficacy**

Dawn Massey

Fort Walton Beach, Florida

At Florosa Elementary in Florida, conversations similar to the one in Scenario 2 can consistently be observed. The principal bends over backwards to make time for teachers to work together to close student learning gaps using formative assessment data. Teacher data teams meet to discuss individual and grade level data, and more importantly, they use the data to develop instructional practices for small groups. Dawn and members of the leadership team regularly attend the teacher meetings to learn from the conversations and offer support for the teachers' instructional plans. Dawn readily states that she is not the smartest person at the table. She learns about the needs of the students from her teams, and she provides them what they need to get the job done.

After one of the last faculty meetings of the school year, a teacher met with Dawn to share that she thought the formative assessments for her grade were easier this year as compared to previous years. When Dawn inquired as to why she thought this, the teacher responded that the students had done so well, much better than last year. Dawn reminded her of the data chats on the formative assessments, and the level of rigor in the materials the team was using with the students. She talked with the teacher about the instructional strategies the team implemented targeted to student needs. The teacher listened quietly and asked, "Are you saying that we should take credit for the improved scores?" Dawn was quiet and waited, and then the teacher said, "*Yes! Yes, we should take credit for the results! What we did worked!*" Dawn agreed and reiterated the connection between quality instruction and improving student learning.

Sometimes teachers need help in making the connections between what they are doing in the classroom and the learning outcomes for students. Once they see firsthand that their practices influence student learning, their sense of collective efficacy grows. Having a trusted leader who helps teachers connect their strategies to improved student achievement builds trust and collective teacher efficacy.

As you endeavor to strengthen trust in your school, think also about how efficacy is built. I have provided five ways to facilitating collective efficacy below.

Five Ways to Build Collective Teacher Efficacy

1. Provide affirmation to teachers that you believe that they are capable and you have confidence in their ability to improve learning for all students, not only in their own classrooms, but across the entire school.

2. Share information about the effects of collective teacher efficacy with the staff and talk with them about what you plan to do to help facilitate building collective efficacy. Ask the teachers what they might do to strengthen collective efficacy and support them in their work.

3. Provide scheduled and structured time for teachers to work together to analyze data and determine the impact of their efforts on learning of all students, and then to collaborate on the most effective strategies to move all students to mastery.

4. Empower and support teachers implementing instructional strategies that are designed to improve the achievement of all students.

5. Celebrate and recognize improvements in student learning and make explicit connections between the learning and the adult actions that preceded the learning. This will provide concrete examples that their work matters and that they can impact learning for even the most struggling leaners. Make these connections as often as possible and share them so that teachers begin to see and believe that they can make a difference when they work collaboratively in service to all students.

In the next section, the focus is on building trust and leading instruction using courageous candor.

USE COURAGEOUS CANDOR

As a consultant working with principals in states with new, more rigorous teacher evaluation instruments, one of the things I hear most often from principals is how uncomfortable they are having conversations with teachers about performance. This is a result of the many years of nearly all teachers being ranked as excellent or highly proficient on past evaluation systems. Now, with new evaluation expectations in place, leaders are being asked to provide more accurate ratings, using student achievement results to justify their ratings along with specific evidence from multiple classroom visits. This shift in performance evaluations, and calls for greater accountability for the ratings, requires both courage and candor on the part of the principal.

Veteran leaders convey that they have become more skilled at having these conversations over time, but that they still have some uneasiness before they begin. New leaders, overwhelmingly, express that this is one of the hardest parts of their job. Some leaders suffer more anxiety than others, but they all have a level of fear when it comes to speaking candidly with teachers on issues of underperformance.

There is agreement in the literature that effective feedback is goal oriented, tangible, transparent, actionable, user-friendly, timely, and consistent. It is designed to prompt a change in performance or lend affirmation for the continuation of certain practices. Using courageous candor during feedback sessions is necessary if a change in practice is to occur, and improvement in teaching and learning is to be realized.

Courageous candor is disciplined and thoughtful. It is based on clear expectations and nonjudgmental evidence of teachers meeting or not meeting those expectations. Feedback conversations with teachers should be grounded by the instructional vision and indicators in the teacher evaluation instrument. These provide the language needed to make points clear, relevant, and consistent. The most important thing to keep in mind is that evidence, not judgments, will lead to successful feedback sessions with your teachers. Avoid editorializing, and provide evidence to the teacher to facilitate their self-reflection and conclusion drawing. This will open the opportunity for an effective collaboration for improvement.

This approach may be difficult because principals are primarily seen as evaluators and are expected to provide "expert advice" to their teachers to improve instruction, as opposed to sharing nonjudgmental observations for the purpose of professional learning. I have provided a chart below to illustrate the difference between judgmental and nonjudgmental feedback.

Judgmental/Editorial	Nonjudgmental/Evidence
• Your class was out of control.	• During the observation, I counted 6 students out of their seats, 4 students on their phones, and 5 students with their backs to you while you were teaching.
• Your questioning techniques were flawless.	• Your questioning techniques were effective, as you used cuing, probing, and wait time. You called on volunteers and nonvolunteers, and you held students accountable for answering and listening to the answers from their peers.
• The lesson was too easy for students, and they will probably fail the state test if you don't raise the rigor.	• During the lesson, you asked students to read and respond to comprehension questions from the text. There were no questions asking them to draw inferences or to analyze the text, which are requirements in the seventh-grade standards.
• You seemed to be in a bad mood during the lesson.	• During the observation, I noted that you told John to "shut up" and that you refused to answer Sue when she asked what she was supposed to be doing.

Being candid with teachers becomes more effective when specific evidence is shared and used to start a conversation about what comes next for improvement. The evidence should not be sugar-coated, nor should you make excuses for the teacher when the evidence is shared. This takes courage, but it will lead to a conversation about what occurred in the classroom and what might come next to spur improvement. You might ask the teacher to provide her thinking about how to proceed. What strategies is she considering? It is more effective for teachers to come to their own solutions based on the evidence you share, because then they own it, and will be more likely to change their practice, as opposed to being told what to do by the "expert."

The Principal Profile below highlights the work of Tommy Thompson and his effort to improve teaching and learning at his school by providing candid, actionable feedback to his staff.

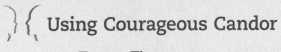 Using Courageous Candor

Tommy Thompson

New London, Connecticut

Tommy Thompson subscribes to a number of important leadership values that precede and ground his work with teachers to improve instruction. First, Tommy strives to communicate with great clarity on what effective teaching looks like at New London High. He thinks it is unfair to ask teachers to hit a moving target.

With the instructional expectations clearly communicated, and a genuine interest in helping teachers improve their practice, Tommy has laid the groundwork to enable candid conversations with teachers about teaching quality and opportunities for improvement. Tommy's motto is to keep things simple so that things are clear. "We focus on what we are teaching, how we are teaching it, and whom we are teaching." These three questions guide every conversation he has with staff about instruction.

One of the nonnegotiables at New London is the use of common formative assessments. Teachers have daily planning time to analyze the data and develop instructional strategies designed to meet the needs of the students revealed in the data. When these practices are absent from the teaching process, Tommy follows through and provides candid feedback to teachers to get them back on track. He may ask a series of questions, and offer a number of supports to ensure that the required practices are being used. He is direct, he uses nonjudgmental data to support his conversation, and he sticks to his expectations for performance, while simultaneously offering support and guidance for improvement.

(Continued)

(Continued)

To further support teachers Tommy created a Summer Institute and encouraged all teachers to participate, but he specifically invited teachers who were struggling to help them meet expectations. The goal of the Institute was to increase teacher effectiveness via the use of video and coaching. Teachers spent 1 hour teaching summer school students and 3 hours planning collaboratively, analyzing data, and viewing footage of themselves instructing students. Like great athletes break down film, teachers were viewing their practice alongside instructional coaches, which ultimately helped them improve their practice.

However, when a pattern of noncompliance or poor implementation of the expected strategies continues, Tommy creates charts and visuals with the observation data over time to illustrate exactly where the problems are, and he shares the data with the teacher in post observational conferences. His color-coded charts, using red, yellow, and green highlights, clearly illustrate which strategies were observed at the effective level, which ones were progressing, and which ones were absent or not implemented effectively. This color-coded data provide a solid foundation for a candid conversation with teachers about necessary next steps and types of support needed.

The final leadership practice in the trust cup is handling mistakes well, in order to fail forward and build a high trust culture. This practice is the focus of the section which follows.

 ## FAIL FORWARD: EXPECT AND HANDLE MISTAKES WELL

Even with the best intentions and strong work ethic, people will make mistakes. That includes you. It is how you respond to and handle mistakes that will either build or destroy trust. Handling mistakes well will also enable you to learn and "fail forward," as every failure, mistake, or misstep is an opportunity for growth. Research by Lee and colleagues (2001; as quoted in Pury & Lopez, 2010) published in *The Psychology of Courage*, presents evidence that organizational performance is negatively impacted in two scenarios, both when managers fail to explicitly state that mistakes would be forgiven and when employees were punished for making mistakes. In both cases, employees were less likely to experiment with new programs or take risks to innovate. In contrast, people who worked for managers who explicitly communicated their willingness to work through mistakes, as opposed to punishing individuals who made them, tend to be more innovative and willing to extend themselves and their best thinking to their work (Pury & Lopez, 2010).

This research is very useful for school leaders trying to build trust. A culture of exploration, collaboration, and empowerment is not possible if the members are fearful and anticipatory of punishment when mistakes happen. No one likes to make mistakes and no one wants to be responsible for something going wrong. But, the fact is it happens in all facets of life. Most teachers strive for excellence, and they are very hard on themselves when they make mistakes or when things do not go as planned. They need to trust that mistakes are expected and will be forgiven and that they are viewed as opportunities for learning.

> People who worked for managers who explicitly communicated their willingness to work through mistakes, as opposed to punishing individuals who made them, tend to be more innovative and willing to extend themselves and their best thinking to their work.

Teachers develop their conceptions about making mistakes by watching how you handle them. Handling mistakes well is not a difficult thing to do, but it requires courage and integrity. Handling mistakes well starts with self. When you make a mistake do you

- Acknowledge when you have made a mistake and take responsibility for it?

- Apologize to those that have been hurt or affected by your mistake?

- Develop and implement a plan to make things right and repair the damage, as well as prevent a re-occurrence of the mistake?

- Reflect on what can be learned and use the lesson to fail forward?

- Move on and get over it?

Keep in mind, you are always under the watchful eye of your staff. They will learn how mistakes will be handled when they see you make one. Your behavior serves as a model for your team on how they should respond when they make a mistake. When you acknowledge your mistake, accept responsibility for it, repair the damage, learn from it, and move on, you are sending an important message about how you want your team to handle their mistakes, and how they can expect to be treated by you when they make a mistake. Do not miss the opportunity to learn and fail forward.

In addition to following the example you set, teachers need to be told explicitly how you will handle their mistakes. They need to know they will not be yelled at, admonished publicly, humiliated, or unfairly punished. It is a good idea to have an established process or protocol, like the one shared earlier, in place for handling mistakes and to follow it consistently. This will lower anxiety and build confidence and trust in your school.

In the Principal Profile which follows, April Brown shares a story that reinforces the power of having a process when mistakes are made and she exhibits great courage in making the mistake public and failing forward from it.

Principal Profile

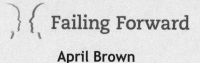 Failing Forward

April Brown

Chester Upland, Pennsylvania

April Brown, principal of Main Street Elementary in Chester, PA, provides an excellent example of failing forward. In the spring of 2015, in the first year of her principalship, she experienced every principal's worst fear—a lost child. She was notified by her staff that a 6-year-old, nonverbal autistic boy was missing from the school. Of course, everyone at the school set out to find the child, but when they could not locate him, the district office was notified as well as the parents and the local police department. Everyone from the superintendent, to central office staffers, to teachers were searching the area around the school to find this child. After hours of frantic worry and fear, the child was found several miles from the school in a creek bed by passersby. He was soaking wet and confused, but was unharmed.

Back at the school, the parents and central administration convened to go over what happened and determine where mistakes were made. Immediately, April accepted responsibility and apologized to the parents and her supervisors. She said the breakdown was her responsibility and she would do whatever it took to pinpoint where the breakdown occurred and to rectify the situation with tighter security and layers of check points among staff so that it never happened again. At the faculty meeting soon after, April apologized to the staff and told them she was accountable and responsible for the safety of students at Main Street, and that she would be working with them to develop new procedures for transitioning students from location to location and from teacher to teacher.

April faced repercussions from her supervisor, as did the teachers who were involved. But, the mistake was handled well by her, and it resulted in trust being built between April and her staff because of the way she handled it. She followed the protocol described earlier. She readily acknowledged the mistake and accepted responsibility for it. She apologized to those who were harmed. She developed a plan to make things right and prevent a reoccurrence. She followed through on her plan and involved everyone in implementing the plan, and she moved on.

This required leadership courage, and as her staff bore witness to it, they began to trust. They also saw firsthand how mistakes would be handled and how they should handle mistakes in the future. Although this was a stressful situation for all, the staff was able to fail forward and grow due to the leadership of their principal.

CONCLUSION

I began this chapter by stating that courageous school leaders build trust, not by accident or happenstance, but intentionally and with purpose, and I explained that trust is the first Cup of Courage because trust is the foundation upon which everything else is built. Without trust, courageous leadership is not possible. I have shared the research on trust in schools and the leadership practices that are necessary to have a full trust cup. Additionally, these practices; co-creating and communicating a shared instructional vision, leading adult learning, building collective teacher efficacy, using courageous candor, and failing forward by handling mistakes well were illustrated in the stories of the five principals in the Principal Profile sections to provide clarity of how each one plays out in real schools.

Chapter Summary

Key Points

- Building trust enables courageous leadership.

- The four types of everyday courage must be activated in building trust in schools.

- Trust serves as a glue and a lubricant to school success: a glue binds people together and a lubricant serves as a grease for organizational operations.

- The consequences of distrust are that teachers become unwilling to take risks and do not extend themselves to colleagues.

- Micromanagement, directives, and lots of rules are present in cultures of distrust.

- When distrust takes hold, it spreads and multiplies.

- Trust is a lever for the development of collective teacher efficacy.

- Teachers need to trust their leaders in order to cope with new standards, new evaluation systems, and new accountability systems.

- Courageous practices which build trust include:
  1. Co-creating a shared instructional vision and goals
  2. Leading adult learning in relation to the instructional vision and goals
  3. Building collective teacher efficacy
  4. Using courageous candor
  5. Failing forward by handling mistakes well

- Trust is the foundation for courageous leadership, and it enables strong leadership in the accountability and risk-taking domains of everyday courage.

Chapter 3

Learning Activity: Courageous Practices to Build Trust

Keep ~ Stop ~ Start

This activity will take you back to the chapter to do some reflecting and planning on how you might strengthen trust in your school. Each of the five practices are listed in the chart below. For each courageous practice, you will place a response in the boxes labeled KEEP, STOP, and START. In the KEEP box, you will list the practices you have in place that based on your reading are effective in building trust in your school. In the STOP box, you will reflect on your reading and record any practices that you currently use that are damaging trust in your school, and you plan to stop using them. Finally, in the START box, you will select one to two specific courageous actions you will take based on your reading that you will start doing to build trust in your school.

Courageous Practices	KEEP	STOP	START
Co-create and communicate a shared instructional vision and goals.			
Lead adult learning.			
Build collective teacher efficacy.			
Use courageous candor.			
Fail forward—handle mistakes and failures well.			

Cup of Courage: Accountability Practices

Blame and victim thinking are so ingrained into the fabric of our society it's hard to find a role model anywhere who simply practices personal accountability in all things.

—John Miller

OVERVIEW OF ACCOUNTABILITY

Accountability has become a dirty word in education as a result of the No Child Left Behind legislation passed under the Bush Administration. Government mandated accountability aimed to punish schools by imposing sanctions and consequences on schools that failed to meet the requirements. It created victims and generated a victim mentality among both struggling and successful schools. It has not proven to be overly effective at improving low-performing schools, and it did not motivate or solve underperformance issues in student subgroups organized by ethnicity, poverty, special education, and/or language. It required the removal of school leaders in hundreds of designated turnaround schools across the country with mixed results. Some schools experienced remarkable improvements and others languished with low test scores, high staff turnover, and dysfunctional school cultures. The wide variability in the results of federally mandated turnarounds is a testament to the ineffectiveness of punishment-based external accountability systems.

External accountability is the accountability imposed on schools and districts by state and federal lawmakers and departments of education. These accountability systems often include blaming, punishing, sanctioning, ranking, reporting, and embarrassing low-performing schools. These external mandates have led to cultures of compliance as opposed to cultures of commitment to excellence in the classroom. What has resulted is excuse making and victim thinking in struggling schools, as opposed to empowered, collaborative problem solving to help move from low to higher performing.

> External accountability is the accountability imposed on schools and districts by state and federal lawmakers and departments of education.

ACCOUNTABILITY THAT WORKS

Accountability should not be a dirty word in education. In the true sense of the word, it is an attitude, a belief, a personal commitment, and most of all, a choice of people within an organization. It is a desire to take responsibility for results, and it requires an affinity for taking action toward solutions to problems. It is empowerment and ownership when it is not mandated by external forces. The most powerful accountability begins at the personal level and spreads to a collective group from inside of the organization.

Richard Elmore postulates that internal accountability is the real lever to school improvement. Internal accountability can be described as the ownership and responsibility for results that members of a team share. Staff members feel personally accountable to each other and to their students. They choose to honor the commitments they make to each other including creating quality lesson plans, utilizing a formative assessment process, or preparing data reports for team analysis. Internal accountability depends on genuine connections among staff and a collective moral purpose for the work. In schools where internal accountability is strong, individuals are personally committed to improving student learning and to their team's success. There is a culture of interdependence and accountability for results at the individual and school levels. As a result, team members give their very best effort to contribute to the organization's success, and there is an identifiable cohesion to the work toward a greater good.

When internal accountability is high, a school culture moves from one where the work of the organization is the sum of the individuals to one where the work of individuals is shaped and determined by the collective expectations, values, and commitments made with one another (Elmore, 2005). This type of culture cannot be accomplished by mandates and top-down directives. It has to be inten-

Internal accountability can be described as the ownership and responsibility for results that members of a team share. Staff members feel personally accountable to each other and to their students.

tionally cultivated by activating the four domains of everyday courage; moral courage, intellectual courage, empathetic courage, and disciplined courage, which set the stage for building an accountable culture.

In December 2015, President Obama's signature marked the reauthorization of the 1965 ESEA as ESSA: Every Student Succeeds Act. The biggest shift in the focus of accountability from NCLB to ESSA is the redistribution of power back to states and a more holistic approach to accountability. For over a decade, the federal government has attempted to drive student achievement, especially for the most vulnerable student populations, by way of sanctions tied to a narrow definition of student success. ESSA offers a chance that accountability systems will evolve under state control to include growth models and application of multiple measures that extend beyond state test scores. In fact, ESSA requires all states to establish an accountability system based on multiple indicators including (Cook-Harvey & Stosich, 2016):

1. academic achievement;

2. another academic indicator, which must include graduation rates at the high school level;

3. English proficiency; and

4. at least one other valid, reliable, comparable, and statewide indicator of school quality or student success. (p. 12)

Educators nationwide are hopeful that the accountability systems of blame and punishment will fade and a new age of growth-oriented measures will emerge; however, the future of ESSA and accountability systems are uncertain given the election of Donald Trump and his selection of Betsy DeVos to lead the Department of Education.

LEADERSHIP PRACTICES THAT FILL THE ACCOUNTABILITY CUP

In this section, the specific practices of leading and building an accountable school culture are described. As you read, you will find that these practices overlap with the practices in the trust cup, and that they are interdependent with the practices in Chapter 5 on risk-taking. Internal accountability cannot be built without trust, and trust will be lost if people do not have shared commitments and values. Each of these is required in order for leaders and teachers to engage in risk-taking. During your reading, begin to note how these practices interrelate with the practices in the trust cup and keep them in mind as you read Chapter 5. It will help you synthesize the separate parts for an overall understanding of everyday courage in schools.

The leadership practices that contribute to the development of an accountable culture include embracing personal accountability, building a sense of collective accountability, and implementing reciprocal accountability. Building an accountable culture also relies on facing and acting on brutal facts by listening to staff on the effectiveness of their work and of your leadership. All of these practices are reflective of what the research tells us about effective leadership in high performing organizations, and they are powerful levers for creating an accountable culture that will help you reduce excuse making, blame, and victim thinking in your school. Implementing these practices will require the activation of all four domains of everyday courage.

The following section focuses on the first leadership practice in creating an accountable culture-embracing personal accountability. This practice sets the foundation for the other practices in this cup.

EMBRACE PERSONAL ACCOUNTABILITY

School leaders sometimes find themselves in situations that are not of their choosing. But those who practice personal accountability realize they have a choice about how to view the situation and how to take ownership of finding a workable way out of it. Personal accountability involves assessing the reality of the situation, exploring viable options, clarifying the desired outcome, and deciding on the best first step and taking it. Personally accountable leaders seek out supportive, action-oriented people to collaborate with and enlist their assistance when needed.

Conversely, people who have a victim mentality facing the same circumstances respond with "Why me?" "How am I supposed to deal with this?" " I cannot handle this on top of all of the other things happening to me right now." They might also seek out others for sympathy and a listening ear for their complaints and laments. They spend all of their energy thinking of reasons why they cannot solve the problem, as opposed to expending that energy to solve the problem and meet their objectives. They might also stick their head in the sand or pretend the situation does not exist.

All the while, teachers are watching and learning about how to handle the tough situations they are facing. You determine the mindset your teachers adopt. Will it be one of ownership, empowerment, and engagement? Or, will it be one of blame, complaints, and excuse making? Unfortunately, we have all worked for or been witness to cowardly leadership and the effects it has on a staff. People will fly under the radar, work from a compliance mindset, and hold back their best ideas. Accepting personal accountability is foundational for leading a school to success. This means taking ownership and responsibility for the success of all students and accountability for the growth and development of staff.

In an accountable culture, courageous leadership also involves holding others accountable for their actions and performance. Not just sometimes or when it is convenient, but all of the time. Leaders must commit to making it a habit. Holding people accountable is actually a gift to the entire staff. Not holding all staff members accountable all of the time and consistently, is a punishment and the best performers will not tolerate it.

Finally, personal accountability from the leader first, followed by the staff, creates tremendous opportunities for growth, renewal, and positive collective action. It builds organizational trust and spurs collective accountability in an organization.

In the Principal Profile that follows, April Brown exhibits personal accountability. Her work helps illustrate how embracing personal accountability contributes to creating an accountable culture.

}{ Embracing Personal Accountability

April Brown

Chester Upland, Pennsylvania

April Brown faces tremendous challenges at Main Street Elementary, and the challenges began day one of her principalship in 2014/15. During the year prior to her appointment, the former principal left amid questions about test security after being there less than 2 years. She was replaced by a substitute principal, and then a consultant principal took over until April was hired. The school culture was one of fear, distrust, and dysfunction. Student achievement was extremely low with large percentages of students lacking proficiency in reading and math. The majority of the staff needed support with effective instructional practices, classroom routines and structures, and guidance with implementing new reading and math programs adopted by the district. A number of teachers lacked a sense of collective efficacy and did not demonstrate high expectations for all students. All of these factors contributed to the high staff turnover.

As you may recall, I began this discussion by saying that school leaders sometimes find themselves in situations that are not of their choosing. This is definitely one of those situations. A first-year principal stepping into a job where every aspect of the organization needed support is not ideal. It could have been overwhelming, frustrating, frightening, and paralyzing, but April was not overwhelmed or paralyzed. Quite the contrary. She embraced personal accountability for the situation, and committed to finding a workable way forward.

April's core values and commitment to every child in her school is at the heart of her personal accountability for results. She is relentless in her endeavor to improve school for all students. She believes it is her responsibility, regardless of prior events at the school, regardless of the learning deficits of students, and regardless of staff turnover.

She sets the example for teachers to embrace accountability by her actions and words. She teaches students when she visits classrooms. She disciplines students in the hallways. She attends teacher meetings, and she holds regular leadership team meetings where everyone is expected to own the results. She does not blame, make excuses or play the victim. She focuses on doing all that can be done in order to move the school forward. She builds accountability by being personally accountable.

Personal accountability is a strong lever in creating an accountable culture. It is even more powerful when coupled with reciprocal accountability, which is the focus in the next section.

 USE RECIPROCAL ACCOUNTABILITY

Reciprocal accountability means that for every increment of performance we expect of others, we have an equal responsibility to provide them with the capacity to meet that expectation. In essence, if we are going to hold you—a teacher or principal—accountable for something, we have an equal and commensurate responsibility to ensure that you know how to do what we are expecting you to do. In short, high demands are accompanied by high support.

Highly effective teachers understand the concept of reciprocal accountability and practice it in their classrooms. They have high expectations for their students and demand much from them. They readily accept that they have a responsibility to provide effective instruction, quality feedback toward a learning goal, emotional support, encouragement, and engaging resources in order to achieve the expected outcomes. They work with students individually, in small groups and whole group to meet their learning needs. They do not expect students to be proficient on skills and content that they have had no opportunity to learn. They have a reciprocal relationship with the students and each is accountable for the outcomes.

Now let us examine reciprocal accountability with the principal–teacher relationship in mind. Effective principals understand and recognize their teachers as individual learners. When changes in practice are required, they ensure that their teachers have opportunities to learn and practice before they are held accountable for proficiency. They provide a variety of learning opportunities for teachers and strive to understand all teachers' strengths and growth areas in order to support them in their implementation of new strategies. They work with teachers individually, in small groups or teams, and they work with the faculty as a whole, to ensure that there is clarity and opportunity for questions along the way. They provide feedback and guidance over time for continued growth and refinement of the new practices. They do not expect proficiency without multiple opportunities to learn and refine practices.

Additionally, effective principals focus on results in student learning. They communicate long and short term goals, usually in a school improvement plan, and they monitor progress throughout the year toward the goals. They intervene early when they identify teachers in need of assistance and they provide quality feedback accompanied with coaching, mentoring, modeling, or other means of helping teachers achieve the expected gains. They participate in what Stephen Fink, Executive Director of University of Washington Center for Educational Leadership, calls learning-focused partnerships. These partnerships do not rely on top-down directives and orders from above to spur learning and achievement. Rather, they rely on collaboration between and among teachers, principals, and central office administrators to support each other in their learning to improve instruction and thus improve learning for all students in their care (Fink, 2011).

In the Principal Profile that follows, Ashton Clemmons illustrates how she uses reciprocal accountability to improve teaching and learning, while building an accountable culture for results.

Principal Profile

 Reciprocal Accountability

Ashton Clemmons

Guilford County, North Carolina

Ashton Clemmons understands the importance of reciprocal accountability. When she arrived at Brooks Global Magnet School, she was an experienced principal with a reputation for results. Her previous school, Oak Hill

Elementary, was a nationally recognized Title I school that served a student population that was 99% economically disadvantaged and 99% students of color from immigrant families, as well as African-American, mid-eastern, and Latino families. Much was expected from the teachers at Oak Hill, and much support was provided so that they could do what was being asked of them. As a result, they developed quality, standards-based lessons, analyzed student achievement data, made adjustments to meet the needs of every child, and maintained high expectations for performance.

When Ashton arrived at Brooks, she learned that because Brooks was a good school, with good results and satisfied parents, there was no pressure or urgency to improve. But, she was sure that the school could better their best and provide a highly rigorous instructional program that would benefit all students, including the students who heretofore have not been consistently successful.

Her first task was to help teachers move away from textbook-driven instruction and replace it with standards-based lessons. This was quite a shift for a staff who relied on traditional teaching formats, straight rows, worksheets, and page-by-page coverage of the textbook. At every faculty meeting, Ashton modeled a standard-based lesson. She guided the teachers through unwrapping a literacy standard and analyzing the implications of the grade level standards toward the twelfth-grade anchor standard. During grade level PLC meetings, she asked the teachers to bring in student assignments, and she guided them through a process to analyze the alignment between the assignment and the requirements in the standards. She facilitated sessions whereby the teachers revised the original assignments to match the rigor and skill required in the standard. She constantly provided feedback and support so that teachers could meet her high expectations.

Finally, Ashton established a learning partnership with them, as posited by Stephen Fink. She has provided the teachers the skills and tools necessary for them to do what was being asked. Her high demands were accompanied with high support. Now teachers are held accountable for providing students with high-quality lessons based on the North Carolina academic standards, and they have learned, by watching Ashton, what it means to be a partner in learning with their leader.

This kind of accountability, high demand with high support, as well as the personal accountability demonstrated by the leader, are the prerequisites to building collective accountability which is discussed in the following section.

 ## CREATE COLLECTIVE ACCOUNTABILITY

Collective accountability is a key characteristic of high-performing organizations. People in these organizations accept responsibility for results, and they work cooperatively with each other to achieve at high levels. They have strong connections with each other, and they are responsible to each other. Reaching goals is a joint enterprise and no one is successful, unless all of them are successful. Collective accountability is born from the personal accountability demonstrated by the leader, and the reciprocal accountability they embrace. It cannot be directed, ordered, mandated, or forced. It is the personal choice of the members, and internally driven.

In addition to modeling personal accountability, there are other leadership actions you can take to grow collective accountability in your school. One way to grow collective accountability is to be mindful of the conversations you have with staff when they are facing a problem. Susan Scott (2002), author of the Fierce Conversations books recommends that leaders reflect on their conversations to determine if they are catalysts for change and accountability or if they further entrench people in fear, blame, and victimhood. Scott argues that the missing link to collective accountability is conversations with teachers that speak directly to the heart of an issue, activating their curiosity to uncover the truth and connecting them with others to problem solve. She reminds us that attempts to mandate accountability from the top down is an effort in futility.

In your efforts to develop collective accountability in your school, it is important to understand what will derail your work. When teachers come to you with challenges they should resolve on their own, you should avoid; solving the problem for them, or discounting their opinions as non-valid, flawed or wrong. These actions will keep you and your staff in victimhood where people feel disempowered and disengaged from the work.

Instead, try engaging people in a conversation that plants the seeds of accountability for results. When a team of teachers requests your help with a problem, refrain from solving it for them because that is the fastest way to get them out of your office. Take a few minutes to help them accept responsibility for solving their own problems and empower them to take control of the challenges they face, while remaining empathetic to their needs.

Having this type of conversation will empower people and encourage them to take control of the challenges they face. This cannot happen if you come to their rescue when they hit a road block or if you get caught up in their story. You must be empathetic and nonjudgmental. Do not share how you would handle it or how you have previously been in a similar situation. This is theirs to solve and resolve. These conversations, along with your personal accountability and use of reciprocal accountability, will inspire trust and collective accountability, and ultimately risk-taking, which will be discussed in the next chapter.

Principal Emily Paul has successfully built a sense of collective accountability at her school in New Orleans. Her work is chronicled in the profile that follows.

Principal Profile

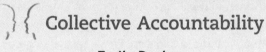 Collective Accountability

Emily Paul

New Orleans, Louisiana

Emily Paul, principal of Good Shepherd Catholic School in New Orleans has successfully built an accountable culture in her school. Her success is due mainly to how she views accountability and the core values she follows when working with her staff. Emily subscribes to the "we," not "me" philosophy of leadership. She stated during our interview, that successful schools are born from unity, collaboration, and diverse thinking. Emily makes clear that she has always been a leader who wants to hear from the staff. She wants them to be empowered

(Continued)

(Continued)

and contribute to the decisions that are being made. She believes that effective school leaders guide, supervise, motivate, and empower teachers in order to create a school culture of shared accountability and ownership of both successes and failures.

In the beginning of her tenure, she says it was hard for the staff to understand that she wanted them involved. She worked with the teachers both as a faculty and individually to help them recognize that they did indeed have the problem-solving skills and leadership qualities to find solutions to the school's most vexing problems. She encouraged risk-taking and reassured the staff that failure was ok. It just meant they had to go back to the drawing board.

Finally, the teachers at Good Shepherd have been empowered to make decisions, work as a team, solve problems, set goals, and own results. Emily and her staff, "plan the work and work the plan," when it comes to improving learning for all students. This collective accountability was built at the hand of a wise leader who follows the "Musketeer Mentality," of "One for all and all for one." She holds people accountable and refuses to accept less than excellence in the classroom, but she has achieved this by sharing leadership, listening to their ideas, helping them plan and execute interventions, make decisions about schedules, curriculum and instructional practices, as opposed to top-down directives and mandates. Emily said during our interview, "empowerment is so important because teachers will never find their wings if they are not given the opportunity to soar."

In summary, building an accountable culture requires courage from the leader. It entails stepping up to embrace personal accountability in situations that are beyond your control, and developing a mindset that problem-solving and deliberate action can forge a path out of it. Personal accountability is the first step in eliminating blame and excuses from your culture, and it prompts others in your school to adopt personal accountability as well.

Creating an accountable culture is also built on the use of reciprocal accountability. Leaders have an obligation to their teachers to provide support through professional learning, feedback, and space for mistakes and refinement when requiring new practices. They understand that high demands must be accompanied with high support.

These practices, personal accountability and the utilization of reciprocal accountability, help to create a sense of collective accountability among teachers and staff members where they collectively own the challenges they face and together they work to solve them. They do not blame students, each other or you for their challenges. They work cooperatively and interdependently for the success of the entire school. Creating this kind of accountable culture does not come easy. It requires courage on a number of levels, most notably disciplined courage to see it through and empathetic courage as you work with staff.

The final practice in building an accountable culture is facing the brutal facts. If you cannot or will not face the brutal facts of your current reality, any kind of accountability is not possible. Facing brutal facts is the focus of the next section.

 ## FACE THE BRUTAL FACTS

Strong, courageous leaders do not wear rose-colored glasses. They do not engage in denial of the facts, and they do not pretend all is well when clearly things need to change. Courageous leaders embrace the facts and use them as opportunities for growth, empowerment, and improvement.

Jim Collins, author of the best-selling book *From Good to Great*, presented the concept of facing brutal facts as a characteristic of organizations who made the leap from good to great. Since the publication of the book in 2001 organizations worldwide, including educational institutions, have applied his thinking to their improvement agendas. Facing the brutal facts is an act of everyday courage for school leaders as it takes guts to face the realities in your organization—hear from staff on how they see things, look at data and know that students are being underserved, listen to parents on their perceptions of the school, and receive feedback from supervisors that indicate concerns.

As I present the practice of facing the brutal facts, it is important to note that this is not about looking at student achievement data per se; rather it is about facing the facts about your leadership, the culture of the school, and the impact of the work that both you and the teachers do every day. While data-driven decision making is certainly important to your school's success, facing brutal facts is much deeper, and quite frankly requires greater courage on your part.

One of the greatest leadership flaws in any organization is the failure to see things as they are and deal with the current reality of a situation. Oftentimes, this is due to the emotional connection that you have with the current practices and culture of the school, or it is because recognizing the truth will mean that your ideas have failed to produce results. Either way, it is deadly to the culture and performance of your people to wear blinders to the reality of things. Failing to see the facts, choosing to ignore the facts, or glossing over the facts leads to the loss of your credibility, the loss of trust from your staff, and the loss of an opportunity to excel. Leaders must create a culture where trust is high and people are free to share their thoughts and feelings about how things are going and the barriers they see in the way of success, and you must be able to hear the truth from them.

Collins suggests four practices for leaders to create a culture where the brutal facts are shared and confronted. I have listed these practices and provided examples related to everyday courage for school leaders under each one:

1. **Lead with questions, not answers.**

   Whether you are analyzing data with staff, attending PLC meetings, or talking with teachers informally, it is a great idea to lead conversations with questions that will generate information you can learn from. Ask questions focused on the big picture, such as "Is our school working for all students? How do we know? What should we do if things are not working for all students? The bottom line here is that you must ask the questions and be prepared to truly hear the answers, and most importantly act on the facts to improve.

2. **Engage in dialogue and debate, not coercion.**

   In a culture that faces the brutal facts, professional dialogue and debate are encouraged and supported. Teachers and principals alike should have passionate discussions based on facts where every voice is heard, every idea is considered, and everyone is motivated to respond effectively to the current reality.

3. **Conduct autopsies without blame.**

   When bad decisions have been made or mistakes have happened, it is important to engage in what the military calls an after-action analysis. In this analysis, all team members assume positive intent of everyone involved and approach the discussion from that perspective. Your guiding questions should include the following: What could we have done differently? What should we have considered, but did not? What can we all learn from this as we go forward? What has to happen to rectify the situation as it stands now? Leave blame out of the conversation. Blame leads people to retreat and cover up. Problems cannot be solved when that happens, and they are likely to be repeated in the future.

4. **Build "red flag" mechanisms.**

   Schools generally have red flag mechanisms in place to ensure the safety and security of their students: from active shooter drills, to infectious disease alerts, to weather threats. But at other times, the reality of a situation may call for immediate action related to student learning. Red flag actions may be initiated during a data team meeting where assessment data reveals that very few students have learned a required skill that is critical for their future learning. Or, red flag actions are needed when the results on benchmark or state assessments reveal a particular grade level is not showing proficiency at the same levels as other grades. These situations require immediate action, as the student learning hangs in the balance, and they require multiple perspectives and voices to determine the best course of action.

In summary, confronting the brutal facts goes deeper than simple data-driven decision making, and it takes courage to create a culture where the truth is shared and heard by all. High-performing organizations find that confronting the brutal facts empowers them and lifts them to higher levels of achievement. They do not become dispirited or weak as a result of confronting the brutal facts: They become stronger and more resilient.

In the profile that follows, Stan Law of Indianapolis provides an inspiring example of facing and dealing with brutal facts in a challenging and complex context.

}{ Face the Brutal Facts

Stanley Law

Indianapolis, Indiana

Stan Law is the principal of Arlington Junior/Senior High School in Indianapolis Public Schools (IPS). The school first came to notoriety in 2012 when it was placed on Indiana's list of 10 "drop-out factories" after 6 consecutive years of being rated an "F" school by the state as a result of abysmal student performance and unacceptably low graduation rates. The state turned operations of the school over to a charter company to turn it around. But, they too failed to bring positive change to the school, and they gave the school back to the state midway through their contract. The mayor of Indianapolis appealed to the state Department of Education requesting the return of the school to IPS, and in the summer of 2015, the request was granted. In July 2015, Stan was selected to lead the turnaround at Arlington.

When Stan arrived to Arlington, he was under a great deal of pressure to improve results quickly. There was pressure from the community, the district, and the DOE to turn things around. He had a local newspaper reporter "embedded" in the school on a weekly basis to document the turnaround. He had a disenfranchised staff with low expectations for student performance, and a student body who had little to no hope for a bright future.

Stan only had 6 weeks to learn all he could before school started in the fall of 2015. He spoke with community members, teachers, students, and parents. And the brutal facts came rushing in like white water rapids. He learned that students had no understanding of the requirements for graduation, which explained why only 40% were graduating on time.

Additionally, he learned that pass rates on the state tests were as low as possible with 0% passing seventh and eighth-grade math and English. And sadly, things were not much better for the upper grades. Most leaders would have found the reality of this situation overwhelming and most leaders would have been reluctant to take on such a challenge, but not Stan. He felt it was a terrible travesty that students did not have a good school to attend and that they were being forced into a life of second class citizenry because they were not graduating with the skills they needed to further their education or get a good job.

Stan made the decision to tackle the graduation brutal facts first. He gathered his team and shared the gravity of the situation. He did not spend time blaming the staff. He led with questions and a desire to understand, which enabled a productive dialogue. Together, they examined every transcript of students who should be graduating. During our interview, Stan shared that they had about 80 students in the senior cohort and only 22 were on track to graduate. The remaining 58 students had not taken the necessary coursework, and/or they had not passed the required state tests. This was a red flag moment at Arlington.

These were brutal facts, and the staff, with the support of Stan, created action plans for each student, which included individualized programs to get them into the courses they needed to graduate. For some, it involved schedule changes, for others it meant online courses on top of their schedule, and for others it included summer school, Saturday school and after school support. They dealt with a lot of push back from the students and parents, but they were not deterred. Stan appointed a graduation coach who kept him informed, as well as the school counselors on the students' progress. Many of the staff rallied around a "do whatever it takes mindset" and worked with students during lunch, stayed late in the evenings, and met students in the mornings to help them meet the requirements.

With all of the issues and the complexity of the situation, Stan has not become dispirited and his resolve has not been broken. At no point has he put on rose colored glasses, stuck his head in the sand or swept the brutal facts under the rug. He has confronted the issues, making mistakes along the way and learning from them. Stan's guiding principle was and still is, "Together we can, and together we will!"

(Continued)

Facing the brutal facts on behalf of students has led to strong relationships with students and their families, it has built trust between and among the staff and administrators, and has led to a resiliency among the entire school community.

Early data show promising results for the first year. Well over 70% of the students will graduate on time, and upwards of 30%-40% of seventh and eighth graders will pass the state tests in math and ELA. Although this is significant improvement, Stan is quick to say the work is just getting started. By facing the brutal facts and tackling them one at a time, the students at Arlington now have a reason to hope for and achieve a brighter future.

CONCLUSION

Creating an accountable culture is complex work, and it takes courage to make it happen. The courageous practices of embracing personal accountability, utilizing reciprocal accountability, building collective accountability, and facing the brutal facts are necessary for strong leadership in schools. These practices require fortitude and persistence, as well as deep introspection. They can be developed through deliberate practice and the activation of moral, intellectual, disciplined, and empathetic courage.

Chapter Summary

Key Points

- Accountability has taken on a negative connotation due to NCLB legislation, but it should be viewed more positively by school leaders.

- The leadership practices that contribute to the development of an accountable culture include embracing personal accountability, building a sense of collective accountability, and implementing reciprocal accountability.

- Internal accountability depends on genuine connections among staff and a collective moral purpose for the work, which leads to shared ownership for success.

- Effective principals engage in "learning-focused partnerships" with teachers, and when changes in practice are required, they ensure that teachers have opportunities to learn and practice before they are held accountable for proficiency.

- Collective accountability is born from the personal accountability demonstrated by the leader and the reciprocal accountability they embrace. It cannot be directed, ordered, mandated, or forced.

- One of the greatest leadership flaws in any organization is the failure to see things as they are and deal with the current reality of a situation.

- Jim Collins, author of *Good to Great*, provides leaders four practices for creating a culture where the brutal facts are confronted:

    1. Lead with questions, not answers.
    2. Engage in dialogue and debate, not coercion.
    3. Conduct autopsies without blame.
    4. Build "red flag" mechanisms.

Chapter 4

Learning Activity: Building an Accountable Culture

Building an accountable culture starts with personal accountability. In this activity, reflect on a difficult situation you are in now or have recently been involved in. Think about how you first responded in this situation. Read the descriptors below that compare the accountable mentality to the victim mentality. Put a check next to the questions that best reflect what went through your mind during your challenge. If your actions align with the accountable mentality, you have the foundational skills to build an accountable culture. If your actions align with the victim mentality, you have some work to do on yourself before you can build an accountable culture. Your first step is to keep these questions handy the next time you face a challenge and try using them to guide you to a workable solution. Accepting personal accountability for situations that are not of your choosing requires that you embrace the challenge and accept that you are responsible for finding a workable way out of it.

The Accountable Mentality: Things Happen Because of You		The Victim Mentality: Things Happen to You	
What is the reality of this situation? What is happening?		Why is this happening to me now?	
What are my options?		Who is responsible this?	
What is the best possible outcome?		Can I wait this out?	
What is my best first step to reach that outcome?		What do people expect of me? Don't I do enough?	
Who can I enlist to help implement a solution plan?		Who can I find to console me?	

Cup of Courage: Risk-Taking Practices

You cannot swim for new horizons until you have courage to lose sight of the shore.

—William Faulkner

OVERVIEW OF RISK-TAKING

Risk-taking can be described as undertaking a task in which there is a lack of certainty, potential consequences, or failure. Risk-taking is an essential aspect of leadership today, but being a risk taker has negative connotations because it elicits thoughts of danger, hazards, and potential harm. At the core of risk-taking is fear: fear of being fired, fear of failure, fear of success, fear of looking foolish, fear of disappointing others, fear of being ridiculed, and the list goes on. Taking risks involves confronting the fears and the uncertainty, and moving forward with an action you know is in the best interests of students and the school. Recall the discussion in previous chapters about overcoming fear and leading from a courage mindset. Risk-taking builds courage and serves as a spark to the courage center in the brain as discussed in Chapter 1.

Taking Smart Risks

Leaders who take smart risks understand that there is a difference between taking calculated risks and risky behavior. Smart risk-taking is grounded and maintains a favorable balance between benefits weighed against potential consequences.

Risk takers thrive in complex work environments, and they get things done. They set trends that others follow, get positive attention from supervisors as "go-getters," and most importantly, implement solutions that make things better for the school community. This is in contrast to non-risk-takers who delay making decisions, stick to traditional processes and procedures, and inadvertently protect the status quo. Thus, nothing of significance changes and nothing innovative ever happens in their schools. Leaders with an aversion to risks often find they are buried beneath issues and situations demanding their attention, and they have little or no time for instructional leadership and relationship building with staff. Fear-based leadership and playing it small stifles innovation and change for improvement.

How to Take Risks

Risk-taking generally starts with exploring solutions to long-standing problems that are getting in the way of success. A new idea or concept sparks a creative plan to solve the problem that has not been previously tried or considered. A risk taker engages in dialogue with members of the team, possibly the leadership team, to weigh the benefits and consequences of an action. Risk takers ask themselves and their team questions like: What's the worst that can happen? What have we got to lose? Are the benefits worth the risk? If it fails, how hard will it be to recover? They are aware of the potential negative consequences, and they are willing to accept them if the benefits of the action are worth it. They prepare for failure and success, and they embrace the process as they learn and grow.

Once an idea is in motion, you must be prepared for things to go wrong. This means you must be flexible, continually innovate, and problem solve along the way with members of the team. You cannot possibly predict everything that might go wrong before your idea is implemented. Risk takers are creative leaders who nimbly adjust to ensure the success of their innovations. Risk takers also anticipate threats. They know that threats may come from within and outside of the organization. They expect and prepare for doubters and haters, and they activate their courage to weather the storm until the end. Risk takers also develop great instincts for future risk-taking as they gain more experience and learn from their successes and failures.

> Risk takers are creative leaders who nimbly adjust to ensure the success of their innovations.

The Benefits of Taking Risks

Risk takers are learners. They learn valuable lessons by taking on tough challenges and stretching themselves by taking risks that pose potential consequences. They accept that they must change to grow and that failure is part of success because of the lessons learned from it. They succeed in doing things differently because they adapt as they go and they reap the rewards of improved results.

Although risk takers acknowledge the risks, they focus on future success. They are confident that a new master schedule will foster improved student learning. They believe that new pedagogies will result in student mastery of complex skills. They have faith that their new coaching and feedback techniques will facilitate teacher growth and development. They see students and teachers winning via improved performances, and they see themselves winning because of the personal growth. They maintain their optimism throughout the process.

Leadership is about finding new and better ways of doing things, even when things are going well. In fact, it is very tempting to tread water when things are going along well and the waters are smooth, but this is a mistake. Risk takers are always looking for new ideas, new concepts, and new strategies that will improve things. They face their fears and venture from the shore to discover new horizons and see what may lie ahead. They risk failure and uncertainty to reap the benefits of what is currently unknown.

Finally, your willingness to take risks builds your internal strength and grit. The lessons learned while taking risks lay the foundation for the next set of risks you decide to tackle. You will be better positioned for success each time risks are taken making the next time a little less riskier. With each courageous act in risk taking, you become more knowledgeable, confident, and open to new risks for school improvement.

LEADERSHIP PRACTICES THAT FILL THE RISK-TAKING CUP

In this section, the specific practices of risk-taking are described. As you read, reflect back on the practices in the previous chapters on building trust and creating an accountable school culture. The practices in the risk-taking cup are intertwined with those practices, and all of them together are necessary if you hope to fully activate your everyday courage and lead from a courage mindset. Also, remember the four essential domains that frame the three Cups of Courage: moral courage, intellectual courage, empathetic courage, and disciplined courage. Each of the practices in the risk-taking cup will rely on your utilization of all four courage domains.

The leadership practices in risk-taking include leading with core values centered on equity, excellence and inclusion for all students, innovating and designing for new and better learning experiences, fearlessly focusing on what matters most, and modeling resiliency when disappointments occur. All of these practices are well grounded in the research on effective school leadership. Similar to Chapters 3 and 4, each of the practices in the risk-taking cup are illustrated with real stories from practicing principals to help deepen your understanding of risk-taking and how to get started taking calculated risks to improve your school.

The next section begins the discussion on leadership practices necessary for risk-taking with a focus on leading with core values centered on equity, excellence, and inclusion.

LEAD WITH CORE VALUES

Leaders are constantly faced with choices as they strive to lead more courageously. The choices might include safety or growth, blame or responsibility, mediocrity or excellence, or cowardice or courage. Staying true to your core values and an inspired vision for the future moderates risk-taking as a calming, steadying force in your work.

School leaders are compelled to adopt and lead with core values centered on equity, excellence, and inclusion for all students. Not only do the new national standards have a strong and explicit emphasis on these values, but it is a moral obligation to do so. It is a requirement for success. You must possess unswerving beliefs in the inherent ability of all students to achieve in a rigorous academic environment. It requires that you vigorously promote the core beliefs with everyone in the school community, and act when injustices or unfairness occurs. For example, if you know that students of color are underrepresented in gifted and honor classes, you must act to correct it. If you notice that one student group is over identified in special education classes, you must act. If you see that discipline procedures result in disproportionate suspensions for a certain group of students, you must act.

This can be scary and risky depending on the school community, which is why a clearly defined set of core values is needed, and why activating your courage is so important.

> Being able to choose the courageous path and take reasonable risks means making choices that are aligned with ones' most basic core values and principles so that there is harmony among what you know is right for all students, what you are doing, and who you are being (Warrell, 2009, p. 276).

Many leaders post their personal core values in their office and talk about them often with teachers, parents, and students so that everyone in the school community understands the principles that guide their decisions. There is great value in doing this because when decisions are made, people have learned what is behind the decision. They know what you stand for and what you are hoping to achieve for the students and staff. When you act in accordance with your core values, stakeholders are less likely to question or second guess you, even if they do not agree with the decision.

Additionally, when you have publicized and shared your core values, you will hold yourself accountable for acting in accordance with them. It is very difficult to declare your core values to a school community and then make decisions that violate the core values. This will damage your credibility and make it difficult to build trust. If you do not intend to honor your core values, then do not share them with others.

Consider the earlier discussion on moral courage in Chapter 1. Moral courage is the backbone to risk taking and leading in accordance with your core values. At times, you may be asked to implement new mandates, fall in line with political decisions, continue long honored traditions, or give favor to individuals or groups for various reasons. Every school leader faces these dilemmas from time to time, and they are laden with risks and challenges. But, values-driven leaders have a ballast that provides stability and clarity during these times. Courageous leaders rely on their core values to help find a way to implement mandates in a manner that benefits students. If there is no way to align the two, and what you are being asked to do harms students or undermines what you are trying to accomplish at your school, then you have to be willing to share your objections and have conversations with involved parties, as it relates to your core values. And ultimately, as Tommy Thompson said in Chapter 1, you have to be willing to be a short timer, if you are being asked to do something that you believe is harmful to students or staff. At the end of the day, you have to sleep at night knowing you have done everything you can to provide your students an excellent education. Perseverance and adaptability are key skills for leaders who stick to their core values in times when it is difficult to do so.

When you live by your core values, you give other people permission to do the same. They will declare their own core values to others and feel empowered to make decisions guided by them. Consistent core values build a strong organizational commitment to the work and binds people together for a greater purpose.

The Principal Profile that follows provides multiple examples, from the leaders featured throughout the book, on leading with core values centered on equity, excellence, and inclusion.

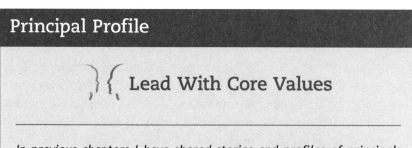

Principal Profile

}{ Lead With Core Values

In previous chapters I have shared stories and profiles of principals from around the country to illustrate the courageous practices in action. Their stories were matched to a specific Cup of Courage and

specific leadership practice to illustrate examples of courageous prac-
tices in action in real schools. However, in this section, I found it
difficult to choose just one principal to serve as an example of leading
with your core values. Each and every principal I spoke with for this
book, as well as the many principals I work with around the country,
are guided by a set of core values centered on equity, excellence, and
inclusion. These core values serve as their moral compass, and every
decision they make can be linked back to these core values, as illus-
trated in the following pages.

Tommy Thompson's core values are highly personal, as he links his work back to his four school-age sons. He believes every student in his school should have access and opportunity to achieve his or her life's poten- tial, and he wants for each of his students what he wants for his sons. If the services provided to the students are not acceptable for his chil- dren, then they are not acceptable for the New London High students.

Walter Perez, who you will read about in this chapter, grew up in poverty in South America and attributes his success to the dedicated teachers who helped him. His guiding light is framed by his experience, and he ensures that the students in his care have the same opportu- nities he was provided by teachers willing to do whatever it takes to ensure success.

Sara Manzo is grounded by a core value of inclusivity. Because her school receives students from outside of the district, she believes that all stu- dents should have ownership of their school and be treated as valued members of the school community, both socially and academically.

April Brown and Stan Law are guided by the core value that all stu- dents, regardless of current academic proficiency, deserve an educa- tion that is rigorous and provides them with options and opportunities in life. They lead from the belief that all adults in a school are respon- sible to serve students with excellence, dedication, and a passion for their success.

David Sauer is guided by the core value and belief that powerful liter- acy skills are the key to lifelong success for all students, and although

(Continued)

(Continued)

football and athletics are king in Texas, and his school won the Division III state football championship, David firmly believes that a school's academic program is the true determiner of its quality.

Regardless of how these principals articulate their core values, they all include an agenda of equity, excellence and inclusion for all students; all really means *all*. They lead their schools with clarity and purpose around these values, and they take calculated risks to make things better for all students.

The next section focuses on the practice of embracing innovation and design thinking to solve complex problems in the way of student learning.

 EMBRACE INNOVATION AND DESIGN THINKING

Leaders often hear the calls to become a "change agent" or are prompted to "challenge the status quo" in order to improve and reform their schools. But these terms have become so overused and so cliché that they hardly have meaning any more. Leaders who are truly risk takers are much more than change agents. They are innovators and designers of new and exciting ways to deliver school services that result in improved student learning. They are visionary leaders, who have the ability to cope with the uncertainty that comes with change, and they have the inner strength to see a change through to the end. They begin the change process with innovative thinking and designing that emanate from improving the learning experience for students. This is what lifts a leader from change agent to innovator.

> Leaders who are truly risk takers are much more than change agents. They are innovators and designers of new and exciting ways to deliver school services that result in improved student learning.

Oftentimes, when you read about an innovative school leader, you find they are dubbed innovative because of their acquisition and utilization of technology in classrooms and around the school. Many "innovative" schools have gone paperless and deliver instruction in Goggle Classroom, or they have students engaged in creating apps for iPhones, or using various devices to engage students in real-world learning experiences. All of these instructional advancements are wonderful and necessary to enrich the learning of students. But, innovation and design in leadership is not limited to innovative uses of modern technology in schools. Can a school leader who lacks the capacity to purchase 1:1 devices for students be an innovative leader? The answer is of course they can, and they should, if they hope to keep pace with what is needed for successful school leadership in modern times. Innovation is about people and the way they think. It is not about technology per se.

CHARACTERISTICS OF INNOVATIVE LEADERS

Being an innovative school leader means doing things differently or doing things that have never been done before. Innovators and design thinkers are courageous leaders committed to creating dynamic, highly productive, values-driven schools, who are not afraid to try, fail, and try again when it comes to innovating and designing to improve learning. Innovative leaders are observers and questioners. They see each and every function of a school as an opportunity to improve. They watch how schedules flow, they observe how instruction is delivered, they analyze curriculum guides and academic standards. They watch how busses load and unload, they watch how the office and cafeteria operate, and they carefully craft their ideas from what they see. They ask questions that might include: Why are we doing things this way? If we redesigned the process, what effect would it have on students and the quality of their learning?

Innovative leaders also know how to balance execution and innovation. They manage repeatable processes that deliver solid instruction in every class every day, while simultaneously developing new tools and approaches for improvement. They are excited about doing things differently.

Innovators also understand that innovation never happens in a vacuum. These leaders value and build relationships with the people they work with, and they capitalize on their knowledge and strengths to develop and implement new ways of doing the work. Innovators push people for their best thinking, and they do not hire people exactly like themselves.

They seek to hire a diverse staff who bring different professional and personal experiences to the organization. They are not averse to professional discourse, and encourage debate and dialogue to learn from different points of view and divergent thinking. They do not endeavor to choose the idea of one person over another; rather they strive to co-create a new and better idea that is born from all of the ideas shared. They have the courage to let go of control and empower people to become solution seekers themselves. In this way, they lead from the center of the organization, as opposed to leading from the top.

Finally, innovative leaders encourage innovation at every level of the organization. They attempt to create an innovator's mindset in all of their people because they know that innovation and design thinking will result in creative solutions to their most complex problems. They are not constrained by convention or tradition, and most importantly, they have the wherewithal to see innovations through the change process.

BECOMING AN INNOVATIVE LEADER

Steve Jobs was quoted as saying, "Innovation distinguishes between a leader and a follower." But how does a school leader become an innovator? First and foremost, you must own the role of chief innovator. You cannot entirely delegate the role of designer or innovator to others in your school, no matter how creative or out of the box they may be. However, you can empower people to become innovators and designers and leverage their ideas to improve the school. Second, relationships with people in the school are the key to them contributing to and following through on innovations for improvement. Innovators value their teams, trust them to do good work, believe in their capacity to grow and support them as they learn new things.

Dyer, Gregersen, and Christensen, in *The Innovator's DNA: Mastering the 5 Skills of Disruptive Innovators* (2011), suggest that innovators possess five core skills that include associating, questioning, observing, networking, and experimenting. These skills provide a blueprint for you to begin thinking and acting in new and different ways that will strengthen your work toward improved learning experiences for students. Below is a summary of their thinking.

The first skill is a cognitive skill called associational thinking or associating. In simple terms, you have the ability to input new information and make connections in the brain between seemingly unrelated ideas or questions. This enables you to have innovative breakthroughs.

The remaining four behavioral skills can trigger associational thinking, which enables you to form the building blocks of innovative thinking. They are

- Questioning: Innovators are always questioning to determine why things work as they do. They ask more questions than they have answers.

- Observing: Innovators are intense observers of the world around them. Their observations give them new insights on new ways of doing things.

- Networking: Innovators test new ideas through networks of diverse individuals with different perspectives.

- Experimenting: Innovators are constantly piloting new ideas and trying out new experiences. They spend time visiting new places, seeking new information and testing new approaches in their schools. (Dyer et al., 2011)

These four behavioral skills work in concert to enable associational thinking for innovation and design. Collectively, the five skills make up the innovator's DNA.

BENEFITS OF INNOVATIVE LEADERSHIP

Ultimately, innovative school leaders strive to create new ideas designed to address complex problems that meet the needs of the learners. Design thinkers keep the present and future needs of students at the center. It starts with a desired outcome and is followed with an exploration of a wide array of solutions; some tried and some untried. Leaders who design for students borrow innovations from other professions, including medicine, business, or industry, and they apply the innovations in new and different ways in their schools. They are great listeners, observers, organizers, and conversation leaders around design ideas for improving their schools.

Innovative leaders and design thinkers face challenges and barriers along the way, but they learn and grow from each one, building their strength for the next innovation. As you develop your own capacity for innovation, the members of your staff begin to see innovation as a valued practice and through the example set by you, they begin to develop as innovators as well, subsequently, modeling innovation for their students.

To conclude, America needs innovative leadership in our schools. Although the world has changed dramatically around us, and students are expected to achieve in new and different ways, we have not kept pace in schools. We still try to run schools by tinkering with traditional methods that date back to the industrial age, as opposed to innovating and redesigning the way we work in the modern era. America's competitive edge in the world has come from the ability to innovate. We have an obligation to create schools that foster innovation and design at every level so that our students can continue that edge and lead the nation to greater heights.

The Principal Profile which follows highlights the work of Olivia Amador-Valerio from San Diego. Her innovative leadership provides a clear example of how school principals act as innovators.

Principal Profile

 ### Innovate and Design

Olivia Amador-Valerio

San Diego, California

Olivia Amador-Valerio is an innovative school leader. During her 8-year tenure at Finney Elementary, a school comprised of 79% Latino students with 56% speaking Spanish as their primary language, and 56% of the students designated as economically disadvantaged, she has engineered several innovative processes and designed new and different ways to impact student learning.

Olivia, is relentless in her pursuit of improving the student experience at Finney. She constantly asks questions such as, How are students engaging with their teachers? Do students enjoy coming to school? Are students learning at high levels? Are we doing all we can to support student learning for life success, not just pass tests? For each of these questions and more, she asks herself, "What am I doing to make school better for students, parents and teachers?"

After her first year as principal, she proposed a classroom environment redesign to her staff. She believed this was a good first step as a new principal to both build trust with the staff and introduce new ways of doing business. The goal of the redesign was to create classrooms that were aligned to a rigorous academic culture and to connect students to the resources and instruction they needed to thrive. Specifically, the classrooms included common anchor charts, resource access for students based on their needs, and engaging room arrangements to foster curiosity and hard work.

She then turned her attention to redesigning how teachers were supported in their learning. Olivia developed a plan to increase the time, during the regular school day, that teachers were able to spend with each other and with her to explore, collaborate, and design lessons based on students' needs and the requirements in the Common Core State Standards. She proposed using the school budget to hire three part-time teachers who would work in classrooms on a rotation to allow for a half-day planning for all grade-level teams kindergarten-sixth grade every 8 days. She recruited another principal in the district who would share the three part-time teachers and share the cost. She developed a schedule and rationale for the plan. When she asked the teachers if they would like to have additional time to collaborate and create lessons, of course they agreed. She shared her plan with them, asked for their input, and made it happen.

This idea was born of her intense observing and questioning how to improve teacher learning. She was not afraid to try, fail, and try again. She was experimenting with new and better ways to improve student learning via improving teacher learning. The new structure enabled teachers to engage in professional learning that would actually make a difference in their teaching practices. Olivia was able to

(Continued)

(Continued)

spend extended time with grade-level teams working with them in understanding the new standards and assessments, and most importantly, working with them to learn more about the specific needs of their students, and how to serve them in ways that would accelerate their learning. Olivia demonstrated all of the traits of an innovator discussed earlier.

To further enrich teacher learning and growth at Finney, Olivia wanted to help teachers make the instructional shifts needed to successfully teach the new standards. Again, she demonstrated the traits of an innovator in the way she approached solving this problem. The typical approach of school leaders would be to contact various vendors to learn about their services and hire one to come in and work with teachers. But, Olivia solved her problem differently. She worked with her teachers to review the instructional shifts, and identify specific instructional practices that the teachers would need to learn to align with the new standards. She investigated the services and expertise of various consulting agencies and identified potential partners. In her words, she did not want any "one-hit wonders." Rather, she was seeking custom services over a 3-year period with a consultant who could meet their identified needs and would follow the professional learning cycle.

This professional learning cycle would include helping teachers write lesson plans, conducting model lessons for the teachers to watch, co-teaching a lesson with the teachers, providing quality feedback for growth, and gradually releasing the teachers to implement on their own. Olivia made this selection process totally transparent to the teachers, and together, they decided on the partners as well as the calendar and structure for their professional learning. Olivia was not confined to past practice or traditional ways of arranging for professional development for her staff. She redesigned the process to provide more meaningful and long-lasting professional learning for her teachers.

Finally, Olivia demonstrates the thinking of an innovator by the very words she uses during her conversations with everyone in the school community. I was struck by her use of words such as *agreements, investment, alignment, options,* and others. When I asked her about the meaning of her words, she stated, "I use the language of hearts and minds." She shared that she is very strategic about the words she uses in conversations, such that they align to the goals she has for the students and staff at Finney. For example, instead of asking the teachers how the school budget should be spent, she says, "How can we best *invest our money* to meet the needs of our students?" The term invest denotes a different meaning than spend. She sends the message that the money is there to invest in the student's futures. She also does not like the word *nonnegotiable* when speaking with teachers. In her words, "everything is negotiable!" So, she uses the word *agreements*. She believes agreements are organic, malleable and evolving based on available options, time, and best next steps. Again, using the word agreements sends a different message than nonnegotiables. It encourages engagement and commitment to the work.

Olivia understands that she sets the tone of the school. She strives to build trust and develop strong relationships with the teachers so that they feel a part of the work and feel connected to their colleagues and their students. Olivia believes that intentionally changing the specific words she uses is a key element to creating this kind of culture. This is indeed innovative thinking to the core.

The third leadership practice in risk-taking follows, which is fearlessly focusing on what matters most by having the discipline and strength to reject projects and people that distract the leader's attention from important work.

 FEARLESSLY FOCUS ON WHAT MATTERS MOST

Schools are complex organizations, making the ability to maintain a focus on anything incredibly difficult. But the research is clear about the importance of school leaders focusing on teaching and learning. Vivianne Robinson's research shows us that promoting, participating, and leading teacher learning and development is the highest effect size practice for school leaders (0.84). "This is a large effect and provides some empirical support for calls to school leaders to be actively involved with their teachers as the 'leading learners' of their school" (Robinson, Lloyd, & Rowe,

2008, p. 663). The researchers go on to point out that professional development involves more than principals just arranging for staff to learn.

> This leadership dimension is described as both promoting and participating because more is involved than just supporting or sponsoring other staff in their learning. The leader participates in the learning as leader, learner, or both. . . . The principal is also more likely to be seen by staff as a source of instructional advice, which suggests that they are both more accessible and more knowledgeable about instructional matters than their counterparts in otherwise similar lower achieving schools" (Robinson et al., 2008, p. 663).

In addition, the Wallace Foundation (2012) reports in a synthesis of their numerous studies on instructional leadership titled *The School Principal as Leader: Guiding Schools to Better Teaching and Learning* that principals effective at improving instruction have a relentless focus on instructional delivery and design. They connect frequently and directly with teachers and the classroom. Strong instructional leaders visit classrooms spontaneously 20–60 times a week for the purpose of seeing instruction and talking with the teachers about instruction. These are formative observations about growth for the teachers.

In research reported in *School Leadership that Works*, by Marzano, Waters, and McNulty (2005), the ability to focus was included as one of 21 key responsibilities of effective school leaders. The authors state that the specific behaviors within the responsibility of focus includes among other things, establishing concrete goals for curriculum, instruction, and assessment practices within the school. It is the leader's obligation to keep the staff focused on the goals, and filter out interruptions and distractions that take them off the goal.

These research studies, as well as many others conducted by universities, educational nonprofits, and professional organizations make it clear: The principal's courage and skill to focus on what matters most to students is what separates low and high performers. Of course, there are many people and events that make fearlessly focusing on instructional improvement difficult in day to day school life. It requires having the courage to say no to requests, projects, or events that interfere with or interrupt the teachers' ability to stay focused on delivering quality instruction. It also requires saying no to the people and things that take *you* away from supporting the quality of instruction in your classrooms. When this kind of focus is lost, frustration and fatigue result for you and your staff.

It is no mistake that this practice is in the risk-taking cup. The practices in this cup have potential negative consequences. Fearlessly focusing, and saying no to people and projects that take you away from teaching and learning, might be precarious. But, you have to find a way, whether it's through delegation, creative scheduling of your time, enlisting the support of supervisors, or other means, to maintain a focus on improving learning through improving instruction. Your engagement in leading and promoting teacher learning and building collective teacher efficacy is required for results.

In the Principal Profile that follows, Stan Law demonstrates this kind of fearless focus. His work provides clear examples of how this is done in schools that have competing interests.

Principal Profile

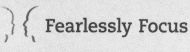 **Fearlessly Focus**

Stanley Law

Indianapolis, Indiana

Stan Law walked into a mess at Arlington High. After a failed turnaround under a charter school company, and years of underperformance on the Indiana state tests, there were many areas needing improvement. The master schedule, guidance services, discipline, safety, budgeting, and staffing, just to name a few. How could Stan manage to fearlessly focus on what mattered most in these circumstances?

The answer is, he focused on what mattered most for that particular time in the evolution of his school. He divided his work into phases by asking himself and the teachers at his school, "What is the most important thing we can do right now?" The answer to that question was to

(Continued)

(Continued)

create an academic school culture. This became his top priority in the beginning of the year. Each of his focused actions on building the culture was a milepost to quality teaching and learning in each class, every day.

In phase one, as he called it, Stan focused on establishing the school as an institution of learning. Students needed to be reintroduced to appropriate school life and regain an understanding of what is and is not acceptable behavior at school. They had to be in class on time, carry books and materials to class, respect their teachers and develop a sense of purpose and hope for their futures. Stan focused his efforts and time on building the culture first, because without an academic culture, instructional improvement was just a pipe dream.

This was not easy, given everything that was swirling around him. But his intentionality and strong sense of purpose behind the effort paid off quickly. By second semester, the culture was starting to change. Students were in class with materials, teachers were able to teach, and students were developing trust and ownership in their school. Although more progress on the culture was needed, it had improved significantly, which enabled Stan and his team to more explicitly focus on improving learning.

In phase two, the team focused on instruction and learning. They worked elbow to elbow with teachers to ensure that quality lesson planning was taking place, and worked with both students and teachers on understanding the state assessments. Stan reviewed lesson plans and gave feedback for improvement. He shared best practice research with the staff and fostered their learning in order to implement new strategies in their classrooms. They began their improvement with student engagement strategies and sound formative assessment practices. At the end of the year, the focus paid to these practices and the changes in the culture, resulted in significant achievement gains and soaring graduation rates.

Stan's ability to focus on establishing an academic culture at the school, and then on supporting and facilitating improvements in instruction are positively impacting the students, teachers and the overall school community. Arlington is quickly shedding its reputation as an inner city drop out factory as a result of the courage and tenacity of the principal to fearlessly focus on work that matters most to student learning and achievement.

In the next section, the courageous practice of modeling resiliency will be discussed. For leaders willing to take risks and persevere through challenges, a resilient spirit is needed. When leaders model resiliency, others follow suit and bounce back from the inevitable disappointments and setbacks inherent in a risk-taking culture.

 MODEL RESILIENCY

Resiliency is defined in the literature as the capacity to rebound or bounce back from adversity, conflict, failure, or increased responsibility (Pury & Lopez, 2010, p. 136). Given the high stakes work in schools today, resiliency is an absolute must to keep people engaged, passionate, and committed to meeting challenging goals. It also is a necessary part of courageous school leadership when risks do not pay off as intended. You cannot create a culture where risk-taking is encouraged without also working on resiliency, because people will stress out and get emotionally weary if they do not learn to keep things in perspective and rebound quickly from setbacks.

Al Siebert, author of the best-selling book *The Resiliency Advantage* (2005), writes that highly resilient people are flexible, adapt quickly to new circumstances, and thrive in constant change. They have the ability to find a silver lining and see redeeming potential or value in most challenges and unpredicted circumstances. As a result, they face disappointments and setbacks with a confidence that they will be able to bounce back and they see the setbacks as temporary and changeable. You might say they have what Carol Dweck calls a *growth mindset* when it comes to facing difficult situations. They believe that with a learning attitude and sound decision making, they can recover and achieve in spite of the disappointment.

In your efforts to take smart risks and encourage risk taking among staff, you must be the model of resiliency when goals are not met or when things do not go as expected. The research clearly points to a few but powerful practices you can employ to build your own resiliency, thereby modeling for your staff how to be resilient people at work.

First, give greater attention to the positive aspects in your work. According to Barbara Fredrickson, author of *Positivity* (2009), one of the determining factors that separates resilient from nonresilient people is their daily repertoire of emotions. She says those who are not resilient feel good when things are good, but when things are not good, they feel horrible and have a hard time pulling out of it. Resilient people experience the same emotional disappointments and they are indeed hard felt, but these emotions do not preclude them for moving forward and seeing the positive, and being grateful for things that are good.

If you have a hard time balancing your emotions when setbacks occur, you have to take control of your thinking patterns. According to Fredrickson, thinking patterns trigger emotional patterns. So, if you curtail your negative thinking by engaging in positive self-talk, you can ward off some of the negative thoughts that impede resiliency. Thinking positive thoughts and developing an attitude of gratitude for what is good and right is a powerful force in helping you rebound more quickly.

Another strategy to develop resiliency is leveraging challenges and disappointments as opportunities to learn. Even when major setbacks occur, there is something to be learned from them. Resilient people ask themselves, What is the lesson here? What is the solution to this? What can I take from this event and apply it to the next one so that things turn out more positively? They look at the pain and the disappointment as an opportunity to grow and evolve. They develop the courage to move toward the pain and embrace their feelings as growing pains that are necessary for improvement. When you embrace these growing pains and model how you learn and evolve from the setback, you help your staff learn how to develop the same resiliency for themselves.

Finally, as you build your personal resiliency as a risk taker and model that resiliency for your staff, you must be mindful to stay in good health and intentionally regulate your own well-being. Healthy lifestyles that include regular exercise and nutritious foods are foundational to both mental and emotional resilience. Getting enough rest, spending time outdoors, eating well, taking mental breaks, and spending time with positive people whom you enjoy, all play a role in keeping you emotionally balanced and personally resilient.

In the final Principal Profile, Walter Perez conveys a distinct and relatable story of the importance of modeling resiliency through the challenges of school improvement.

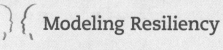

Modeling Resiliency

Walter Perez

Tyler, Texas

Walter Perez is the former principal at T. J. Austin Elementary in Tyler, Texas. (He changed schools in the summer of 2016.) The school serves 460 students in Grades Pre-K to 5. All students qualify for free lunch (with the exception of 18 students who are children of staff members), and 74% are Hispanic, 24% are African-American, with small numbers of white and Asian students. Sixty-six percent of the students are English Language Learners. Austin Elementary was designated by the state as an Improvement Required campus, requiring improved student performance in order to avoid further and more serious sanctions by the state. One of Walter's major challenges was helping teachers try new instructional strategies and building a collective sense of accountability for results, while also building their resiliency.

At the end of the 2014/15 school year, the staff was anxious and excited to receive the data from the Texas state assessments. They felt good about their work and knew that they had worked as a team to make a difference in student learning. When the scores came back showing the that they missed the mark by less than 1 point, they were heartbroken. During our interview, Walter explained that the school was not given credit for a group of higher-performing students because of the calculation formula used to determine the overall performance score. It kept them from exiting IR status.

As difficult as this was for Walter, it was up to him to show resiliency so that his staff could rebound and get back to work. He said he focused on the little success stories and that he found "hopeful indicators everywhere in the data." He said, "At the end of the day, we did what was right for every child." This response is the epitome of resiliency as

(Continued)

(Continued)

described earlier in this section. After he put things into perspective for himself, he had to face his team and support them.

When Walter met with his team, he began the conversation by reminding them that their work was about removing barriers in the way of student success. He also acknowledged the many people who gave it their all and told them, "What you did was phenomenal." He reminded them of all of the good that was done for students throughout the year. He put the attention back on the bright spots and reminded the staff of the lessons they have learned, based on what worked and what did not work. He reminded them, "We don't have the luxury of blaming others. Our work is aligned to the results, and if we want different results next year, we have to accept this, learn from it, and do some things differently."

This approach encouraged the staff to bounce back and see the good in their work. It helped them face the facts, but not be overly discouraged by them. It spurred their adoption of a resiliency mindset, and it set the stage for risk taking in the future.

CONCLUSION

If you want to succeed at risk-taking, you can get started by implementing the courageous practices discussed in this chapter. These leadership practices include leading with core values centered on equity, excellence and inclusion for all students, innovating and designing for new and better student learning experiences, fearlessly focusing on what matters most, and modeling resiliency when disappointments occur.

You must prepare for failure, missteps, and setbacks, but you must also look forward to success, and embrace the process as you learn and grow. Risk-taking builds courage and enables you to stand by your core values, solve problems with innovative thinking, focus on the things that matter most to children, and develop the resiliency for continuous school improvement.

Chapter Summary

Key Points

- Taking smart, calculated risks is necessary for school leaders as a result of the rapidly changing requirements and the speed at which things happen in schools.

- A calculated risk is one that even if it does not work out as you plan, you can easily recover or quickly switch gears to minimize any negative fallout.

- School leaders are compelled to adopt and lead with core values centered on equity, excellence, and inclusion for all students.

- Being able to choose the courageous path and take reasonable risks means making choices that are aligned with ones' most basic core values and principles.

- Innovative leaders strive to create new ideas designed to address complex problems that meet the needs of the learners.

- Innovative leaders and design thinkers face challenges and barriers along the way, but they learn and grow from each one, building their strength for the next innovation.

- Fearlessly focusing on what matters most means saying no to people and projects that take you away from teaching and learning.

- Given the high-stakes work in schools today, resiliency is an absolute must to keep people engaged, passionate, and committed to meeting challenging goals.

- The research points to a few but powerful practices to build resiliency:

  1. Give greater attention to the positive aspects in your work.
  2. Take control of your thinking patterns and engage in positive self-talk.
  3. Leverage challenges as opportunities to learn.
  4. Live a healthy lifestyle.

Chapter 5

Learning Activity: Becoming a RiskTaker—Do Three Things

In this activity, each of the four courageous practices in the risk-taking cup are listed in the first column in the organizer below. For each of the practices, three action steps are provided to get you started in developing your strength in this practice. You may want to select just one or two practices of interest to start with and return to others later. Again, these actions are starter strategies. To become fully engaged and proficient in the practice, you will need to take additional action steps to be determined by you based on your experience with the starter actions.

DO THREE THINGS

Courageous Practice	Action 1	Action 2	Action 3
Lead with core values of equity, excellence, and inclusion.	Post your core values in your office.	Share your core values with the staff at the next meeting.	Intentionally make your next decision using your core values as a guide.
Embrace innovation and design thinking.	Identify a current process or procedure in the way of improving student learning.	Ask many questions about why it is done that way and consider *all* possible ways to do it better. Borrow ideas from other fields.	Hold a meeting with trusted staff to "try out" your thinking, and ask them to think out of the box with you.
Fearlessly focus on what matters most.	Develop a week-long schedule to double the time you spend working with teachers participating in or leading their learning.	Make a list of the things that will likely distract you from following your schedule.	Put an X next to the ones that you will say no to and give the list to your secretary as an accountability partner.

Courageous Practice	Action 1	Action 2	Action 3
Model resiliency.	Implement an attitude of gratitude the next time you face a setback or disappointment. Think about all of the reasons it is not so bad.	Embrace the pain from the setback and make a mental list of what this setback can teach you.	Hang on to humor. Laughing reduces tension and psychologically choosing levity can be incredibly empowering.

PART III

Activating Everyday Courage

Personal Reflection and Development

Before I proceed into the third and final part of the book, I think it is important to review what you have learned so far about everyday courage and why it is an essential component of leadership in schools.

In Part I, the focus was on building a foundation by tracing the evolution of courage to modern day and providing a rationale for why everyday courage is critical to your success as a school leader. You learned about the four domains of everyday courage including moral courage, empathetic courage, disciplined courage, and intellectual courage, as well as how they frame the courageous practices in the areas of trust, accountability, and risk-taking. You further learned that research shows that courage can be learned and strengthened by intentionally engaging in leadership tasks that you most dread or fear. Courageous acts develop courage.

In Part II, the focus moved from foundations to the specific practices of courageous leaders. These practices were organized into three categories or "Cups of Courage," including trust, accountability, and risk-taking. The courageous practices in each of the cups are research based and provide specific actions for you to consider as you endeavor to strengthen your courageous leadership. Additionally, I provided stories from principals like you to illustrate how each of the practices are used in schools by practicing principals.

Now in Part III of the book, I build on the foundation established in Part I, and the specific practices shared in Part II, to provide a discussion and practical advice on activating *your* everyday courage. I will start with a discussion on how you can advance your everyday courage through a courage mindset and engagement in purposeful practice. I also provide easy-to-use tools for you to self-assess to determine the current strength of your courage, and receive recommendations for further development.

CHAPTER 6

Advancing Your *Everyday Courage*

Courage is not something that you already have that makes you brave when the tough times start.

Courage is what you earn when you've been through the tough times and you discover they aren't so tough after all.

—Malcolm Gladwell

Advancing your everyday courage will involve hard work and perseverance. In your reading about the three Cups of Courage in Part II—building trust, establishing an accountable culture, and taking risks—you probably identified specific courageous practices in which you excel. These practices resonated with you as ones of strength and ones that affirmed you are taking the right steps to lead courageously. You may have also taken note of a few practices that you might like to develop to strengthen your everyday courage. Identifying these areas of growth, developing the right mindset to facilitate your growth, and taking steps to realize your growth, is the focus of this chapter.

The quote which follows from Maya Angelou sets the stage for establishing the right mindset to activating your everyday courage. In an interview with *Harvard Business Review* near the end of her life she said,

One isn't born with courage. One develops it. And you develop it by doing small, courageous things, in the same way that one wouldn't set out to pick up a 100-pound bag of rice. If that was one's aim, the person would be advised to pick up a five-pound bag, and then a ten pound, and then a twenty pound, and so forth, until one builds up enough muscle to actually pick up a 100 pounds. And that's the same way with courage. You develop courage by doing courageous things, small things, but things that cost you some exertion – mental and, I suppose, spiritual exertion. (Beard, 2013)

As you read and think about the information in this chapter, keep this quote in mind. Imagine that your everyday courage is the 100-pound bag of rice. To meet the goal of carrying that bag, or fully developing your everyday courage, you must first engage in small steps or acts of courage that prepare you to meet your overall goal. Courageous people are made, one step at a time, one skill at a time, with intentional effort and purposeful practice.

Natural-Born Leaders

For many years, I have heard the phrase "Leaders are born," in leadership meetings about staffing, candidate selection for leadership programs, or conversations about the performance of various principals over the years. People in these meetings make comments like, "She's a born leader," "He's a natural," or "She just gets it." Although I never fully bought into the notion of innate leadership talent, it was not until recent years that I have realized the damage this kind of thinking can have when working with individuals who strive every day to be great leaders. Books by Carol Dweck, Geoff Colvin, Dan Pink, Malcolm Gladwell, and most recently, Anders Ericsson and Robert Pool in *Peak*, demonstrate that leadership is not innate or born. Leadership is learned through experiences, coaching, and feedback. Ericsson and Pool suggest that innate characteristics may contribute to success among those who are just learning a new skill, but that hours of the right kind of practice, as well as a courageous mindset explains more of the variance in performance than any genetic advantage. When people attribute their failures to achieve to innate abilities, they lose the opportunity to excel at something that is important to them, either professionally or personally.

The danger in subscribing to the innate talent theory is that you will never try to develop skills in new areas or encourage others to persist through the challenges of developing new skills. Your thoughts will sound something like, "I'm not a good public speaker, so I should not pursue consulting work." "I'm not good with numbers, so I'll ask the instructional coach to work with the data team." "I don't like confrontations, so I'll ask the assistant principal to tell people to come to work on time." The reality of the situation is that if you face your fears and decide to be a skillful public speaker, or develop a deeper understanding of data analysis, or take charge of professional behavior in your school, you can learn to do it well through practice.

> When people attribute their failures to achieve to innate abilities, they lose the opportunity to excel at something that is important to them, either professionally or personally.

This line of thinking aligns perfectly to Carol Dweck's work with growth and fixed mindsets, which in a nutshell means that intelligence and skill are not fixed or static. Rather, intelligence and skill are malleable and changeable with effort, instruction, and feedback. The same is true for leadership skill. Being an effective, courageous leader does not rely on talent or innate abilities. It relies on a desire to excel, a mindset of confidence and courage, an optimistic outlook, and a commitment to deliberate practice.

Long-term studies reported by Pury and Lopez in *The Psychology of Courage* (2010), support Ericsson's claims. They found that over the past 40 years, research has determined through studies of 646 sets of twins that the large majority of leadership abilities (about 70%) are developed through contextual factors and skills gained from leadership-role attainment. This research disconfirms the belief that leaders are born with innate leadership traits. They found that genetics play a much smaller role in successful leadership (about 30%), with traits such as extroversion, openness, conscientiousness, agreeableness, and neuroticism positively influencing a person's ability to succeed as a leader (Pury & Lopez, 2010, p. 199). The research further confirms that courage and courageous leadership can be developed in any individual who is committed to becoming such a leader. Therefore, anyone can indeed learn to be a courageous leader.

In another study involving over 200 bomb-disposal operators, researchers found that the only factors separating courageous people from uncourageous people were adequate training, good and reliable equipment, high group morale, and live-action experience. The key finding overall was that most of the bomb-disposal operators performed extraordinarily well even though most of them were chosen at random for the position. They were not screened through psychological tests, IQ tests, or personality screeners. The study concluded that virtually all soldiers, officers, and noncommission officers are capable of carrying out this difficult and dangerous work as long as they received specialized training. In other words, anyone can become courageous when certain factors are present (Rachman, 1983).

Courageousness is not some mystical trait that can only be achieved by a small number of special people. It is a trait that anyone can develop. As you have learned in previous chapters, fear will be present, but you can override it, as proven by the neuroscientists at the Wiezmann Institute. Getting comfortable with feeling fear is a critical part of learning how to be courageous. A second critical part is stepping out of your comfort zone again and again until discomfort starts to seem comfortable. Courageous people are simply those who have trained themselves to feel normal during stressful situations. Below are several strategies you might try to override your fear, feel more comfortable being uncomfortable, and build your courage mindset.

Believe in Yourself Without Limits

The first strategy to developing your courage mindset is believing in yourself without limits. Confidence breeds confidence, and improving your leadership is dependent on it. When it comes to how strongly you believe in your ability to conquer challenges and reach goals, boundaries should not exist. It really is a matter of positive self-talk and positive self-attribution. People who see themselves as courageous respond to fear-inducing events more boldly than those who do not see themselves as courageous. You are literally as courageous as you think you are. See yourself as bold and you will behave boldly. This does not mean that you do not have to prepare for events that require your courage, but it does mean that the more you do it, the better you get at it. Courage is created by action. Bold people are just ordinary people who have activated their courage an extraordinary number of times.

Keep Worry at Bay

The second strategy for developing your courage mindset is keeping your worries in perspective. Worrying constantly and staying on high alert will not help you override fear, and it will impede your development as a courageous leader. In fact, high-alert behavior will make you more fearful. Worry can destroy your ability lead effectively because it drains valuable energy, takes away needed focus, causes fatigue and stress, and steals joy. But, how do you deal effectively with it? Researchers asked a group of people to identify what worried them and tracked their worries over time. The important results follow:

- 40% of the worries concerned things that never actually happened.

- 30% of the worries concerned things from the past that could neither be changed nor otherwise influenced.

- 12% of the worries were needless worries about health.

- 10% of the worries were petty worries about unimportant things.

- Only 8% of the worries concerned anything substantial.

- Only half of the 8% involved things that could be controlled or changed. (Cottrell & Harvey, 2004, p. 82)

This is an important study for school leaders. The next time you find yourself unable to focus or lacking energy and motivation to lead due to worrying, ask yourself if your worries fall into one of the categories listed in the study. Force yourself to keep things in perspective by understanding that 96% of the things you worry about either will not happen, are out of your control, are needless, or are really unimportant in the big picture. Highly effective leaders have worries just like the rest of us, but they deliberately refuse to waste their energy stressing over things of which they have no control. Rather, they direct their energy and attention to factors they can control, and they do so with enthusiasm and determination.

> Engaging in actions that can make a difference for others, and fearlessly focusing on the work that matters most, can help you keep your worries at bay and develop the courage you need to succeed.

Research shows that the best antidote for worry is purposeful action. Engaging in actions that can make a difference for others, and fearlessly focusing on the work that matters most, can help you keep your worries at bay and develop the courage you need to succeed.

BE OPTIMISTIC

The final strategy for developing your courage mindset is maintaining an optimistic outlook even when things do not look or feel good. According to Debbie Ford, author of *Courage: Overcoming Fear & Igniting Self-Confidence* (2012), "When you are not complete with the past, you drag it around with you wherever you go, using it as a reference point for who you are, for what you think, for what you believe, and for the choices you make" (p. 144). You have to let go of the patterns from the past that keep you from conquering new challenges and taking the path less travelled. Optimistic leaders allow themselves to use the present moment as their source of inspiration and motivation. They do not allow the voices that cast doubt and instil fear to render them helpless and powerless.

Essential to keeping an optimistic outlook is surrounding yourself with other optimistic people who can keep you on the right track. Their optimism will help you keep your worries in check and have a more positive outlook on things. Also helpful to keeping an optimistic outlook is looking for the best in others and giving yourself credit for what is best in you. You can be your own worst enemy, as 95% of self-talk is negative. This is why positive self-talk is critical to maintaining your optimism and resilience when times are tough (Roselle, 2006).

Martin Seligman, professor at the University of Pennsylvania and author of the national bestseller *Learned Optimism* (2006) has proven that optimists are more successful than equally talented pessimists in business, education, sports, and politics. In one of his studies with Metropolitan Life Insurance Company, he developed the Seligman Attribution Style Questionnaire to sort the pessimists from the optimists during hiring. He followed the performance of both groups over several years. The optimists outsold the pessimists by 20% in year one, and by 50% in year two. He concluded that optimism is a critical factor in keeping people engaged in their work, even in the face of poor results or bad news (Seligman, 2006).

Seligman also tells a story of two sales executives in the shoe business who were sent to Africa to scope out new markets for their products. The first executive wrote back to the company president sharing that the prospects for business were dim because, "No one wears shoes here." The second executive wrote back with a different view. He shared that the potential for business in the area was tremendous because, "No one wears shoes here!" It is easy to see from this simple story why an optimist will outperform a pessimist in any field of work. It is all in the way you see things, which either drives you to seize opportunities or miss them altogether.

Optimism is not easy or natural. It requires focus and re-focus to stay optimistic. As the leader, however, you have significant influence on the resiliency and optimism of the people who work in your school. You have to take the lead to keep problems and worries from taking over your thoughts and actions, which in turn helps teachers do the same. Remember, what you project out is what you get back.

In summary, developing a strong mindset for courageous leadership involves several factors that have significant influence. Developing self-confidence and believing in yourself without limits, keeping worries in perspective knowing that 96% of your worries are without merit, and maintaining an optimistic spirit seeing situations as opportunities to excel and grow are the keystones to a courageous mindset. This mindset is the foundation for moving forward with purposeful action that will build your courage as described by Maya Angelou in her bag-of-rice analogy.

Review the chart that follows and decide which mindset best reflects your mindset during tough times. If you find yourself more on the cowardly side, take note of the traits on the courageous side and commit to transforming your thoughts to align more with the courageous mindset.

Mindset Comparison	
Courageous Mindset	**Cowardly Mindset**
Has confidence and believes in possibilities without limits	Lacks confidence and is a naysayer when possibilities arise
Engages in positive self-talk in challenging situations	Falls victim to self-doubt and fear in challenging situations

(Continued)

Courageous Mindset	Cowardly Mindset
Regulates thinking and avoids spending time on things that cannot be controlled or changed	Allows needless worries to creep in and divert attention away from meaningful work
Expects and embraces new challenges as opportunities to learn	Loses composure and focus when new challenges arise and becomes consumed by the potential to fail
Remains optimistic and determined even when things do not go as expected	Expects that everything that can go wrong will go wrong and gives up when they do

Engaging in purposeful action for growing your courage is the focus in the next section.

THE RIGHT KIND OF PRACTICE

Advancing your everyday courage starts with the right mindset as discussed in the previous section and is completed by engaging in the right kind of practice. Anders Ericsson, renowned psychology professor at Florida State University, has dedicated his entire career to understanding how practice works to help people become the best at what they do. He has found, after 20 years of research, that no matter what your field of work, the most effective types of practice all follow the same set of general principles. In his new book, *Peak: Secrets from the New Science of Expertise*, he writes, "the most effective and most powerful types of practice work by harnessing the adaptability of the human body and brain to create, step by step, the ability to do things that were previously not possible" (Ericsson & Pool, 2016, p. 9). He reminds us that there are no shortcuts in becoming great at anything, but practice can help, and deliberate practice can help a lot! Over the years, he has seen deliberate practice debunk the myths about natural talent and born endowments time and time again. Ericsson considers this type of practice the "gold standard" for lifting people to expert performance.

To get started advancing your courageous leadership, you have to understand the difference between the practice you are probably most familiar with and Ericsson's concept of purposeful and deliberate practice. Regardless of what you have practiced in the past, whether it has been playing golf, preparing gourmet meals, or speaking another language, you have probably followed a traditional way of practicing to improve your skills. Most likely, you started off with a desire to get better in the general sense of the task. You sought out instruction from a knowledgeable source and practiced what you learned over and over. You played many rounds of golf. You prepared hundreds of gourmet meals, or you spent hours listening to and repeating the new language. You improved your skill to satisfactory levels and then you hit a wall and your improvement stopped. You did not become an expert golfer or chef, and you did not develop conversational fluency in a new language. You continued to practice, but the skills stayed stagnant. So, you resigned yourself that you had advanced as far as you could in this area. This is where Ericsson's research becomes so valuable.

Ericsson has found that more and more of the same practice does not make you better at what you do. For example, being a teacher for 20 years does not make you an expert teacher. Becoming an expert teacher takes years of practice on specific skills, such as classroom management, establishing relationships, implementing research-based instructional strategies, creating quality assessments, analyzing data, differentiating instruction to meet students' needs, and so on.

Purposeful practice means choosing one area, one specific skill, and practicing that skill deeply for many hours until it is mastered, then moving on to a very specific next skill and doing the same thing. Over the years, with thousands of hours of purposeful practice completed, your performance will rise to the expert level. This is very different than doing the

> Purposeful practice means choosing one area, one specific skill, and practicing that skill deeply for many hours until it is mastered, then moving on to a very specific next skill and doing the same thing.

same things in your classroom, year after year, and thinking that you are becoming a master teacher. In reality, you are getting really good at the things you started out doing as a first-year teacher. Twenty years later, you are a great first-year teacher!

Let me make the point with another real-life example. Chris Rock is known as one of the greatest comedians in the business along with Richard Pryor and Eddie Murphy. When Rock performed live for his HBO special in 1996, his performance was regarded as one of the finest recorded stand-up comedy performances of all time. *Variety* called the performance one of the truly remarkable hours of comedy ever to air on television . . . transforming Rock from a respected but largely unmarketed standup to the front burner of comedy's future. People raved about Rock's talent and his gift to entertain.

What people did not talk about was the hundreds, possibly thousands, of hours of purposeful practice he put in preparing for this performance. He spent 2 years practicing material in small comedy clubs. He practiced specific content, lines, words, and facial gestures, over and over again, until he believed his routine was excellent. He monitored the reactions of the audience and made notes immediately after the set to make adjustments. He focused on small aspects of each joke and honed his timing, body language, tone, facial expressions, and delivery after each small performance. He was attempting to carry Angelou's 100-pound bag of rice, and he was preparing to do it by first carrying a 5-pound bag, then a 10-pound bag, and so on.

Rock was already a well-known comedian, but he spent the time, energy, and pain to engage in purposeful practice to become one of the greatest comedians in modern times. This takes us back to an earlier question about leadership. Are leaders born or made? Or in this case, are comedians born or made? It is the right kind of practice, not genetics or talent, which produces great performers!

From Purposeful to Deliberate Practice

Now that I have your attention with the notion that experience does not equal expertise, let's examine what distinguishes the right kind of practice for developing your everyday courage. Purposeful practice involves hard work. It is not fun, and it requires intense focus on a few very specific aspects of your overall leadership work.

Purposeful practice has well-defined goals in the specific skills you identify. It involves a series of baby steps, focused on one at a time, toward a greater long-term goal. This way of practicing will take you out of your comfort zone, which is an important aspect of the work. During purposeful practice, you have to anticipate and accept feeling uncomfortable throughout the process.

Effective practice also requires quality feedback. You need a coach, a confidant, a colleague, or a partner to work with you. This supporter must understand your goal and be equipped to provide feedback along the way. Feedback must be based on the goal, and provide you specific information about next steps to move closer to your goal. Getting advice like try harder, do it again, or keep up the good work, does not meet the criteria of quality feedback. If you do not know what to do next to get to your goal, then the feedback is too general and is not helpful to your growth.

Engaging in purposeful practice is important for people who want to be excellent at their work. It transitions you from general improvement to specific improvement on discrete skills. It is based on skill development, not knowledge development. Just as athletes do not train to become a better athlete overall, they train to become a better high jumper, or a better sprinter. You will be working to develop specific skills that are a subset of effective leadership.

Reflect on the practices from each of the three Cups of Courage. Each of the practices represents a subset of the overall skills of courageous leaders. In order to improve and become an expert school leader, you will identify one or two of the courageous practices and work on them one at a time. Your practice will be designed specifically around the aspects of the discrete skill you are striving to develop. For example, if you want to become better at handling mistakes well and failing forward from the trust cup, your actions and practice will be very different from your work in developing the thinking skills to innovate and design new learning experiences for students from the risk-taking cup. All of the courageous practices are connected in that they are essential for activating your everyday courage, but they differ in what it takes to become an expert at each one.

To summarize, purposeful practice is

- based on very clear improvement goals

- intense and demands focus and commitment

- specifically designed to improve discrete aspects of performance

- repeatable over and over until it is automatic

- not very much fun

- highly effective when quality feedback is continuously available

At this point you may be asking, What is the difference between purposeful practice and deliberate practice? Although both purposeful and deliberate practice will accelerate your development as a courageous leader, deliberate practice will provide greater leverage, but is more complex. Deliberate practice requires feedback from expert performers who can provide practice activities designed to improve your performance based on a set of criteria that delineates superior performance (Ericsson & Pool, 2016).

As you engage in practice to develop your overall effectiveness as a school leader, and specifically a courageous leader, you can make great progress even if you do not have an expert mentor to coach you along the way. You will practice purposefully and effectively on very specific aspects of your work, just as Chris Rock did as he prepared for his ground-breaking comedic performance. If you have access to a coach or mentor who possesses superior skills in the areas in which you are working, then your practice will rise to the level of deliberate practice and give you even more leverage in leading courageously. Think about the people in your central office as possible teachers. More than likely, they have come through the principalship and have developed expertise in many critical areas. Once you take the self-assessment in Chapter 7 and identify the courageous practices you want to develop through intense and purposeful practice, you will know who might be a good coach to assist you in your development.

CREATING YOUR PRACTICE PLAN

Advancing your everyday courage is dependent on creating and following an effective practice plan. This begins with an honest self-assessment of the current status of your proficiency on the skills you have learned about in the three Cups of Courage. A review of the essential skills for courageous leadership follows in Figure PII.1.

During your reading about the courageous practices in Chapters 3, 4, and 5, you undoubtedly were self-assessing along the way. This informal personal assessment has given you some idea of where you are strong as well as given you an early indication of the skills you can develop through purposeful practice. To add value to your informal assessment, I have provided you with a more formal tool to self-assess and identify the skills you might

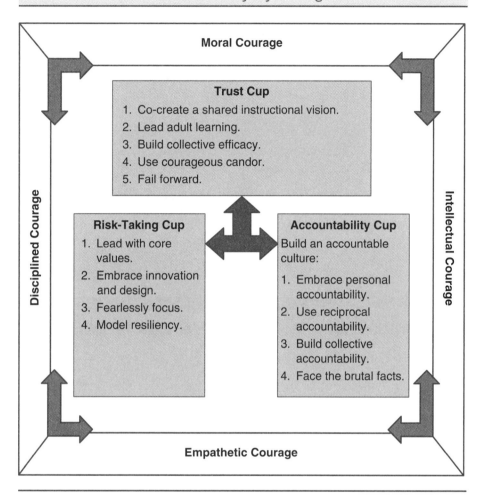

select for growth via a purposeful practice plan. The self-assessment is in the next chapter, along with profiles based on your results and strategy starters for your plan. I encourage you to take the time to take the assessment either online or in Chapter 7 and give deep thought to the results. Ultimately, I hope you will develop a practice plan and enlists the help of a highly successful courageous leader, mentor, coach, or a colleague who can provide quality feedback while you work. This will accelerate your growth and advance your everyday courage.

Conclusion

The purpose of this chapter was to share information and practical ideas to help you get started in advancing your everyday courage. Two main points were shared and expounded upon that are necessary for your development; one, the right mindset, and two, the right kind of practice. Developing a strong mindset for courageous leadership involves several factors that have significant influence: self-confidence and believing in yourself without limits, keeping worries at bay, and maintaining an optimistic attitude. A courageous mindset forms the foundation for purposeful practice. This kind of practice is not so much about helping you reach your potential. Rather, it is designed to help you build your potential. It makes things possible that were previously thought to be impossible. Purposeful practice helps you take control of your destiny and will result in significant growth in courageously leading your school.

Chapter Summary

Key Points

- Courageous people are made, one step at a time, one skill at a time, with intentional effort and purposeful practice.

- Subscribing to the innate talent theory prevents you from developing skills in new areas.

- The research confirms that courage and courageous leadership can be developed in any individual who is committed to becoming such a leader.

- There are three critical elements to developing your courage mindset:

  1. Believing in yourself without limits.

  2. Keeping worries at bay.

  3. Maintaining optimism in difficult times.

- It is the right kind of practice, not genetics or talent, which produces great performers.

- Advancing your courageous leadership depends on the right mindset and the right kind of practice, purposeful practice.

- Purposeful practice is
  - based on very clear improvement goals
  - intense and demands focus and commitment
  - specifically designed to improve discrete aspects of performance
  - repeatable over and over until it is automatic
  - highly effective when quality feedback is continuously available
  - not very much fun

Chapter 6

Learning Activity: Strengthening Your Mindset

In this activity, you will focus on strengthening your mindset in order to ready yourself for purposeful practice in Chapter 7. Think of a challenge you are facing right now that requires that you lead from a courage mindset. For each of the three keystones to a courage mindset listed below, decide on an action you will take to keep this keystone in focus and commit to making it one of your leadership strengths.

KEYSTONES TO A COURAGE MINDSET

Keystone	Action Steps
Believe in yourself without limits.	
Keep worries in perspective.	
Maintain an optimistic spirit.	

CHAPTER 7

Assess and Strengthen Your Everyday Courage

Look well into thyself; there is a source of strength which will always spring up if thou wilt always look there.

—Marcus Aurelius

In Chapter 6, you learned about developing a courageous mindset by believing in yourself without limits, keeping worry at bay and maintaining your optimism. You also learned about the importance of purposeful practice in order to advance your everyday courage.

In this chapter, I shift the focus to self-reflection and assessment so that you can identify specific areas for development that might be included in your practice plan. Engaging in honest self-assessment is a critical first step to developing your everyday courage, and when you commit to making progress on personal leadership goals, it makes you a better leader. It takes a courageous leader to openly admit he or she has leadership weaknesses, and it takes courage to begin to address them by implementing an intense practice plan to improve.

Think about your leadership a year ago, 5 years ago, or more. What kind of leader were you then? How have you changed over the years? What kind of leader are you today? Will you be the same kind of leader a year from now or 5 years from now? Chances are, you are a better leader today then you were a year ago. You have worked hard to develop the skills and knowledge that have contributed to your success thus far. But, even the most effective, highly competent leaders can improve. Your continued improvement and purposeful practice to become a courageous leader for the years ahead is the goal of the work that follows. Acknowledging your fears, identifying the practices that are needed to go forward, and implementing a sound practice plan will result in your development as a courageous leader.

On the pages that follow, you will find the courageous leadership self-assessment. The assessment contains 30 items that were derived from the courageous practices in the three Cups of Courage you have learned about in previous chapters. You may take the assessment on the pages in the book or go online to **www.corwin.com/everydaycourage** to access the survey electronically. If you take the online survey, the score and calculations will be done for you. If you choose the take the survey in the book, you will calculate your own scores using the templates provided. Once you determine your score or Courage Quotient (CQ), you will be provided a Courageous Leadership Profile, which will provide a general overview of your courage in each of the three Cups of Courage—trust, accountability, and risk-taking. The profiles provide an overview of your strengths with potential spoilers, and possible leadership gaps based on the CQ.

Next, you will do a deep-dive analysis to identify the specific practices in each of the three Cups of Courage that you might consider worthy for your practice plan. You will follow a narrowing process to get down to one or two high leverage practices that will help you build your everyday courage. Once these are determined, you may consult the next section, which contains an overview of the topic and strategy starters for each of the practices in all three Cups of Courage. These strategies are designed to jump start your work and provide ideas for your practice plan.

Finally, the self-assessment requires your honest self-reflection on a variety of practices. Please mark the extent of your agreement on each item using the ratings provided on the form. You will respond using strongly agree, agree, slightly agree, disagree, and strongly disagree. Each of the responses carry a numeric value and will be used to calculate your CQ at the end of the assessment.

Courage Quotient (CQ) Self-Assessment: Determine Your CQ

Self-Assessment: Your Courage Quotient (CQ)					
	1	2	3	4	5
Everyday Courage Survey Items	Strongly Disagree	Disagree	Slightly Agree	Agree	Strongly Agree
1. I have ensured that teachers in my school share a clear, consistent understanding of what daily quality teaching entails.					
2. I dedicate most of my time to enhancing the professional learning of my teachers. This may include classroom observations, coaching, attending PLCs, and/or leading professional learning sessions.					
3. Teachers in my school demonstrate a collective belief that together they will impact the learning of all students in the school.					
4. I candidly share nonjudgmental evidence from observations with teachers in order to spur their self-reflection and growth.					
5. I have explicitly communicated to my staff how I view and handle mistakes, including mistakes made by me and mistakes made by them.					

(Continued)

(Continued)

Everyday Courage Survey Items	1 Strongly Disagree	2 Disagree	3 Slightly Agree	4 Agree	5 Strongly Agree
6. Teachers in my school share a strong moral purpose for their work, and they work cooperatively to achieve it.					
7. I model personal accountability for all results in my school—I do not blame, make excuses, or exhibit victim-thinking.					
8. For each expectation I have of teachers, I accept responsibility for providing an equal level of support (guidance, resources and time) for them to meet the expectations.					
9. Teachers in my school have strong relationships with each other, which results in a unified, cohesive team working in service of student learning.					
10. I encourage and expect teachers in my school to share their opinions freely regarding the direction of the school and effectiveness of our practices.					
11. I am constantly looking for ways to improve organizational processes and often create unique ways of doing things.					

Everyday Courage Survey Items	1 Strongly Disagree	2 Disagree	3 Slightly Agree	4 Agree	5 Strongly Agree
12. My decisions are anchored by core values that include excellence, equity, and inclusion for all students.					
13. I am constantly observing and seeking ways to redesign school operations to improve learning for students.					
14. I successfully avoid distractions and maintain a laser focus on teaching and learning.					
15. Even when times are tough, I am able to model resiliency to help my teachers rebound quickly from disappointments.					
16. The instructional vision at my school was a collaborative effort between leaders and teachers.					
17. I am successful at circulating and leveraging teacher expertise in my school to improve the learning of all teachers.					
18. Teachers in my school have a collective belief that their teaching practices have more influence on student learning than any other variable, including poverty and language barriers.					

(Continued)

(Continued)

Everyday Courage Survey Items	1 Strongly Disagree	2 Disagree	3 Slightly Agree	4 Agree	5 Strongly Agree
19. I am comfortable and confident providing post-observation feedback to all teachers in my school, including those who are resistant.					
20. I have demonstrated to teachers, through my actions, that mistakes are to be expected and will be used to "fail forward."					
21. Teachers and leaders in my school share a strong sense of interdependence and accountability for results.					
22. When faced with unexpected, difficult situations, I consistently withhold any reaction in order to implement a process to find a way to a desired outcome.					
23. When changes in practice are expected of my teachers, I ensure that they have ample opportunities to learn, practice and collaborate *before* they are held accountable.					
24. Teachers in my school personally own all student results, not just the results for their own class, subject, or grade level.					

Everyday Courage Survey Items	1 Strongly Disagree	2 Disagree	3 Slightly Agree	4 Agree	5 Strongly Agree
25. I seek honest feedback from staff on my leadership, our culture, and practices and face it head on to learn and grow.					
26. I take risks to improve my school by weighing consequences vs. benefits in the name of student learning.					
27. I have vigorously communicated and publicized my core values to the school community.					
28. I take pride and get personal enjoyment from doing things differently and breaking with past practices.					
29. I am known for saying no to people and projects that take me away from teaching and learning.					
30. When I face disappointments or setbacks, I deliberately focus on what I can learn from the situation and quickly get going again.					

Scoring Your CQ

Using the responses you provided in the self-assessment, place the number value (1–5) in each of the blanks below. For items where you strongly agreed, a value of 5 should be placed in the box. Agree responses carry a value of 4, slightly agree is 3, disagree is 2, and strongly agree is 1. Once all boxes are complete, add the total and write the number in the total box for each of the three Cups of Courage below. Note that the items are not in sequential order.

 TRUST CUP

Survey Items by Number

1.	2.	3.	4.	5.	16.	17.	18.	19.	20.	Total

 ACCOUNTABILITY CUP

Survey Items by Number

6.	7.	8.	9.	10.	21.	22.	23.	24.	25.	Total

 RISK-TAKING CUP

Survey Items by Number

11.	12.	13.	14.	15.	26.	27.	28.	29.	30.	Total

HOW FULL ARE YOUR COURAGE CUPS?

Place a check in the spaces below based on your totals for each of the three Cups of Courage. The score range will help you determine if your cup is full, partial, or low.

Trust   _____   _____   _____

                   Full 45–50   **Partial 31–44**   **Low 10–30**

Accountability   _____   _____   _____

                   Full 45–50   **Partial 31–44**   **Low 10–30**

Risk-Taking   _____   _____   _____

                   Full 45–50   **Partial 31–44**   **Low 10–30**

CQ OVERALL PROFILE

Now you are ready to read your profile based on your CQ score from the self-assessment. Your CQ scores in each cup range from a low of 10 to a high of 50. Transfer your score for each cup to the profile page. Based on whether your cup is full, partial, or low, read the corresponding profile to get a sense for your strengths and potential areas for development. If your cup is full, beware of potential spills or spoilers. A full cup indicates courageous leadership in that area. The profile provides information on these potential spoilers or derailers. For CQ scores that indicate partial or low scores, the profile provides possible explanations for the score and practices for consideration to strengthen your work in this area.

You are encouraged to interact with the text by underlining, highlighting or circling text in the profile descriptions that resonate most with you, or that best describe aspects of your current leadership. There is a "Note to Self" section at the end of each profile for you to record your thoughts on things you want to remember when you develop your practice plan.

 TRUST SCORE _____

Full Cup **45–50 drops**	Leaders with a full trust cup believe their fundamental role is to make the organization better by building the capacity of people. They recognize that a shared vision for quality teaching is essential to building trust and developing people. These leaders see themselves as teachers and learners, first and foremost. They believe that people improve through genuine support, practice, and attentive coaching. They accept mistakes as part of the learning process and they are intentional about helping people learn from the mistakes that are made. When these leaders look at the faces of their people, they see untapped potential in everyone. They constantly look for challenge opportunities for staff members with the intention of building a strong sense of collective teacher efficacy and leadership at every level of the organization. These leaders strive to provide honest, clear feedback based on nonjudgmental evidence, even when the conversations are difficult or uncomfortable. They enjoy developing people to their fullest potential and they understand that the teachers' collective sense of efficacy is a high leverage point for school improvement. ***Beware of Potential Spoilers:*** Leaders who are high scoring in trust can often become very personally invested in the emotions and feelings of their people which may inhibit their ability to lead and hold others accountable. They are passionate about building a supportive culture where teacher growth and development is held in high esteem. The possible spoiler here is that due to their commitment and drive to develop others, they may find it hard to remain objective and lose their candor when it comes to corrective and critical feedback to staff for growth. They may also fail to face mistakes head on as opportunities to learn for fear of deflating or dispiriting their teachers. This may result in the unintentional lowering of high expectations. Being mindful of these potential spoilers can help keep the cup full in this area.
Partial Cup **31–44 drops**	Leaders with partially full trust cups have numerous trust-building practices in place, but have fallen short on several others that may explain the lower score. For example, these leaders may not have established a strong shared vision among staff on what quality teaching and learning looks like at their schools.

Teachers may not have been a part of the development of the school's philosophy of teaching and learning, and they may not know why the principal has asked them to implement certain practices. These leaders work hard to build the capacity of their people; however, they may rely on a core group of people to help lead the school and frequently delegate leadership tasks to this core group. These leaders may not consistently embrace mistakes as learning opportunities and may struggle to model handling mistakes well. These leaders may also be challenged by providing candid feedback to staff for improvement, and oftentimes could be more forthcoming and direct with staff who are seriously deficient or resistant.

Low Cup **10–30 drops**	Leaders with nearly empty trust cups struggle to build a sense of collective teacher efficacy among staff members. They most likely have not collaborated with teachers to create a shared vision for instructional quality, which results in confusion and frustration among teachers. These leaders may also suffer from a lack of confidence in themselves and therefore find it difficult to extend themselves to support the growth of others. This may cause them to overlook the potential in their people. Additionally, these leaders, affected by their own lack of confidence, may only trust a few teachers on their staffs, which leads to negative perceptions and distrust of the leader from the rest of the staff. Leaders low in the trust cup may also be uncomfortable and/or lack confidence in their ability to give honest feedback to staff for growth, especially in circumstances where the person is below standards and/or resistant to feedback. This makes it very difficult to lead for growth and development. Finally, when mistakes occur, the leader may use blame and punishment, as opposed to focusing on lessons learned and finding a way forward. Teachers in schools where trust is low oftentimes transfer to other schools or try to fly under the radar until the leader leaves.

NOTES TO SELF:

ACCOUNTABILITY SCORE_____

| **Full Cup** | Leaders will full accountability cups have a clear vision |
| **45–50 drops** | for the future of their organizations. They understand that accountability from the leader first, can lead to organizational accountability for results and successfully realizing the vision. These leaders rigorously use data to drive their work. They face brutal facts and openly accept personal accountability for missteps, errors, problems, and failures. They openly acknowledge their role when things do not go well, and they apologize to those who were affected by poor decisions. At the same time, they hold everyone accountable to the same high standard of performance for results. These leaders build accountable cultures by having high expectations and providing equal levels of support so that people can meet the high expectations. Accountability is internal and positive. It facilitates continuous school improvement.

Beware of Potential Spoilers:

Leaders who score very high in accountability need to remain mindful of the potential spoilers to their full cup. In their zeal to get things done, they sometimes move too fast and may unintentionally leave people behind. These leaders may not take the time to really listen to input from their people and therefore, miss opportunities for valuable information critical to the success of the work. Finally, because this leader is very high performing in the area of accountability, they lose sight of the fact that their valued teams may not work at the same pace. They share the same passion and dedication, because of the skillful leadership, but they may need a bit more processing time to fully understand and contribute to new ideas. |

| **Partial Cup** | Leaders with partially full accountability cups have some |
| **31–44 drops** | inconsistencies in their actions related to accountability. They may demand excellence from themselves, but not from others in the school, or they may demand excellence from others, but fail to hold themselves to the same high standards. These leaders may not actively seek feedback about their leadership or the culture of the school, as they may not be able to face the brutal facts to guide their leadership. These leaders may have numerous teachers who embrace accountability for results, but a strong sense of collective accountability may be lacking. Finally, these leaders may avoid embracing personal accountability for mistakes, results, or issues, which leads to others in the school doing the same. |

Low Cup	Leaders with near empty accountability cups sometimes
10–30 drops	err on the side of being too nice or too flexible on important issues. They may not be comfortable with challenging people to higher levels of performance. They may not demonstrate personal accountability for results, or they may not hold others accountable for their work. This lack of accountability for self and others makes it impossible to build an accountable culture where a collective sense of accountability exists among all teachers and leaders. There may also be an inconsistent use of data to improve leadership. Decisions are sometimes made based on feelings, fear, status quo, or other nondata-related factors. In schools where accountability is low, blame, excuse making, and victim-thinking are evident.

NOTES TO SELF:

 RISK-TAKING SCORE _____

Full Cup	Leaders with a full risk-taking cup realize that people want
45–50 drops	a leader who has the courage to journey out to make new discoveries. These leaders are keen observers and questioners of current practices and processes. They constantly seek to redesign operations to improve their schools. They are not bound by past practices or historical ways of operating. They are known as creative thinkers and innovators. They are not afraid to try, fail, and try again. However, they take smart risks, in that they weigh benefits vs. consequences in order to make good decisions about which risks are the right ones. They realize that success is found on the other side of change, and they have no problem challenging the status quo for newer and better ways of doing things. Additionally, these leaders are able to maintain

(Continued)

a focus on the things that matter most for student learning, and they exercise great discipline and restraint to keep their focus. These leaders have the courage to say "no" to demands that take them off mission. Finally, risk takers are resilient. They are able to bounce back quickly when setbacks, missteps, or disappointments occur. They can find the silver lining in a failed attempt, and they focus on the lessons learned from it.

Beware Potential Spoilers:

Leaders high in risk-taking are very confident in themselves and the directions they want to go. Sometimes they may be overconfident, however. An overconfident leader fails to plan for and avert problems and issues that could derail the work. They may not listen to or give proper credence to concerns from staff about potential threats to the work. They may believe failure is not possible, therefore they do not develop a plan B, just in case. These leaders are highly capable and skillful; however, they must maintain a keen awareness of all possibilities when taking risks in order prevail. Finally, these leaders must be mindful of the timing and pace of the changes they ask staff to make. Innovative thinking and redesign of outdated processes and practices can transform schools for the better; however, the people being asked to make the changes must have input and involvement in the process. If they are left out, they may become overwhelmed and/or disillusioned.

Partial Cup **31–44 drops**	The leaders with partially full risk-taking cups will step out into the unknown if they are reasonably sure success will result. They will push on the status quo to an extent, but may sometimes back off when challenged by teachers, colleagues, parents or others. This can result in false starts and inconsistent success in implementing new ideas. These leaders also have a clear vision for their organizations, and they attempt to lead with their core values; These leaders may find themselves off focus more than they would like to admit. They are sometimes unwittingly drawn into distractions others could handle. Finally, these leaders may struggle to bounce back after disappointments and may sometimes fail to model resiliency for their teams when things do not turn out as well as expected. however, they may sometimes compromise on their values when faced with opposition. These challenges may also influence the leader's decisions to stay the course on a new initiative or change course on a long-standing practice.

Low Cup	Leaders with near empty risk-taking cups may not
10–30 drops	understand that their teachers want to follow a risk taker who will change things for the better. But, because of fear, these leaders struggle to venture into the unknown. They grapple with decisions that favor the most vocal group or squeaky wheel, as opposed to making decisions that honor their vision, core values, and goals for the organization. They oftentimes lack confidence and, rarely, if ever, share their core values with the school community and staff members. This is problematic because it results in a lack of direction and cohesiveness that is necessary to achieve significant school improvement. It also makes it difficult to lead for change because the lack of a vision or core values forces leaders into a reactive mode, putting out fires and responding to people and requests that may not be related to teaching and learning. Also, these leaders often stick to the safety of the status quo or traditional ways of doing things. They do not actively seek innovative approaches to solve problems, which can frustrate staff members who know there are better ways to operate to meet the needs of students. These leaders find it difficult to focus on the work that matters most, and they are "off mission" more often than "on mission." Finally, disappointments and setbacks spur worry and anxiety, not resiliency. The leader's lack of resiliency can negatively impact the staff, as they will handle disappointments in the same manner as their leader.

NOTES TO SELF:

Before you move on to the next section for a deep-dive analysis of your CQ, take a minute to pause and reflect on what you have learned so far. Review your notes to self and the parts of the three profiles that you underlined and circled. What conclusions can you draw so far? What have you learned about your everyday courage from these results? What parts of the profiles in each Cup of Courage ring true to you? Do you see a pattern of strengths and areas for development? If you scored high in an area, did you take note of the potential spoilers?

Jot down your observations and lessons learned so far, and keep them in mind as you move into the next part of the process.

Lessons Learned/Observations

YOUR CQ: DEEP-DIVE ANALYSIS

Now that you have determined which cups are strengths and which cups are areas for development, you are going to engage in a deeper dive into the results to determine specifically which drops or practices are high and low scored. This deeper analysis will enable you to identify the specific courageous practices that might be targets for purposeful practice. The goal is to zero in on one or two specific practices that you can include in your practice plan for intensive focus and overall improvement.

You will need to go back to your scores in the self-assessment and record the total values (1–5) for the items listed in each box. Each box below indicates the specific practice and the corresponding survey items. Add the two item scores and place the score in the box. Your score range for each box will be from a low of 2 and a high of 10.

For example, if you responded strongly agree (5) to Item 1 and slightly agree (3) to Item 16, you will add these values and place a score of 8 in the box for Shared Instructional Vision. Once all boxes are complete, add the scores and place the total in the total box. The total score at the end of the row will equal the cup scores you determined earlier.

Trust Practices or Drops

Co-create a Shared Instructional Vision Add Items 1 & 16	Lead Adult Learning Add Items 2 & 17	Build Collective Efficacy Add Items 3 & 18	Use Courageous Candor Add Items 4 & 19	Fail Forward Add Items 5 & 20	Total

Accountability Practices or Drops

Create an Accountable Culture Add Items 6 & 21	Embrace Personal Accountability Add Items 7 & 22	Utilize Reciprocal Accountability Add Items 8 & 23	Build Collective Accountability Add Items 9 & 24	Face Brutal Facts Add Items 10 & 25	Total

Risk-Taking Practices or Drops

Take Smart Risks Add Items 11 & 26	Lead with Core Values Add Items 12 & 27	Engage in Innovation & Design Add Items 13 & 28	Fearlessly Focus on What Matters Add Items 14 & 29	Model Resiliency Add Items 15 & 30	Total

Determine strengths and possible targets for purposeful practice.

Strong = 9–10   Medium = 6–8   Weak = 1–5

1. Analyze the results and patterns that emerge as you examine the scores.

2. Circle the practices with the lowest scores.

3. Follow the narrowing process illustrated in Figure 7.1 to identify targets for your practice plan, which includes these questions:

   a. Which is the lowest Cup of Courage overall?

   b. Which practices in that cup are lowest?

   c. Do these practices relate to each other, or are they connected?

   d. Which one or two do you believe are the most important to strengthening your everyday courage?

NARROWING THE FOCUS FOR PURPOSEFUL PRACTICE

FIGURE 7.1   Courage Self-Assessment Items

Lowest Scored Cup(s) of Courage

Lowest Scored Drops

Narrowed to 1 to 2 Focus Areas for Purposeful Practice

AREAS OF FOCUS

Cup_____ Drop(s)_____

Cup_____ Drop(s)_____

Courageous Practices
for School Leaders

Now that you have identified your one or two targets for development, you are ready to build your practice plan. You may use the template at the end of this chapter or you can create a plan format that will facilitate your growth more effectively. In the section below, I have provided a strategy starter for all of the practices which can be used to jump start your work. Locate and read the strategy starters for the practices you have identified for intense practice. Determine if these strategies will be helpful to your development. Decide if you want to implement them as part of your practice and include them in the plan. You may want to use a part of the strategy starter, or modify it to meet your needs, or create strategies with a mentor or colleague. Following your review of the strategy starters, you will be ready to complete the practice plan at the end of the chapter. If you would like to access the online template, you may go to **www.corwin.com/everydaycourage.**

Additionally, you may want to read all of the strategy starters to spark ideas in areas where you are already strong, or use them as they apply to the practices you have identified for development.

Strategy Starters for Purposeful Practice

 ## Trust Cup Practices

DROP 1: CO-CREATE A SHARED VISION OF INSTRUCTIONAL EXCELLENCE

One of the most effective ways to build trust in a school is to include the staff in the development and direction of the work that matters most to them, which is teaching and learning. This does not mean that the leader relinquishes the role of leader, but it does mean that others are made to feel a part and have their voices heard on important issues.

If you have scored low in this area, chances are that teachers do not currently have a clear direction or North Star that guides their instructional practices in the classroom. Most likely they also do not have consistent instructional routines or targets that they strive to meet each day. In this kind of culture, instruction probably goes in many different directions and lacks coherence to address student learning needs.

Establishing a shared vision of instructional excellence is critical to transforming instruction and meeting ambitious student learning goals. Everyone in a school must be clear on the instructional targets essential for all lessons. Knowing the targets helps teachers decide on strategies, procedures and routines in their classrooms which enable them to hit the schoolwide instructional goals.

Finally, when teachers share an instructional vision with their colleagues that they helped create, they have a deep understanding of the why behind the work. This improves engagement and commitment to the goals and it helps them construct the clarity they need to facilitate quality learning experiences for their students. Teacher clarity is one of the critical influences of student learning and has an effect size of 0.75. based on research in *Visible Learning* by John Hattie (2009).

Get Started

To achieve success in co-creating an instructional vision and goals for your school, your background knowledge about instruction is critical. First, do your homework and read contemporary research including *Visible Learning* by John Hattie.

Next, conduct a deep data dive with your leadership team to determine the critical areas of need. Your instructional vision should fully address the root problems standing in the way of success of your students. To guide your data dive, ask and find the answers to questions such as:

- What are our strengths?
  - Subject areas, grades, student groups, specific standards or strands of content, certain skills

- Who is not learning?
  - Grade levels, student groups by gender, socioeconomic groups, ethnicity, special needs groups, or language learners

- What specific standards are a barrier for multiple grades or groups?
  - Reading, writing, math, science, or social studies standards

- What are the root causes or issues that cross grade and subject lines?
  - Literacy skills, analysis skills, writing skills, visual literacy, inductive or deductive reasoning

- Prepare a presentation for the staff making these data points clear.

- Engage the staff in a group discussion on the strengths of the instructional program as they relate to the data. Also, engage them in an analysis of the root causes, but focus the work around factors that are controlled by the school, which includes the instructional program.

- Consider putting the staff into various work groups, each with its own root cause to work through.

- Finally, lead a work session where all staff discuss and contribute to the development of an instructional vision and goals that they will implement to impact the root causes of poor student achievement.

Note: you will recall in Chapter 3 that David Sauer, principal of Mineola High School in Texas, developed a shared vision anchored by improving the literacy skills of all students in all subjects. You may decide similarly, or you may develop a vision based on other skills and knowledge supported in your data. The key is to co-create a schoolwide vision of instructional excellence that is expected in all classes.

DROP 2: LEAD ADULT LEARNING

If a leader demands excellence and results from teachers, they have to be willing to invest the time, money, and people to develop the capacity of staff to deliver excellence. Many leaders will lament the limitations of their people. They don't have the commitment, they don't have the persistence, they don't have the work ethic, and so on. If this is the case, shame on you—the leader!

This is classic fixed mindedness, according to Carol Dweck, respected research and professor at Stanford University. Dweck's studies show that mindset has a tremendous impact on achievement of students and adults alike. Many school leaders agree with Dweck when it comes to how teachers approach their work with students. But, when it comes to their own mindset regarding teachers, some leaders do not apply the same growth mindset principles. They see teachers as born, not made. They do not approach their work with staff from the perspective that any teacher can become a good teacher with the proper coaching, effort and practice. Schools with high-performing cultures and highly productive teams are the result of a strategic approach to developing people.

Get Started

The good news here is that leaders can learn and adapt their thinking and mindset. It is possible to move from a fixed mindset to a growth mindset. The first step, however, is recognizing and calling out your current mindset and developing a plan to change it. Start your reflection by reading *Mindset: The New Psychology of Success* and *Multipliers* (2006). Afterward, ask yourself a series of reflective questions, which might include

- Do I believe that every teacher can be a good teacher with hard work, practice, and good coaching?

- Do I approach my work through the lens of growing good teachers, or do I believe that "teachers are born, not made?"

- Do I systematically search for the natural talents in my staff and put those talents to work for the good of the organization?

- Are talented teachers attracted to my school due to the development opportunities we provide?

- Do I spend time developing a select few team members, or all team members?

Once you have a good understanding of your current mindset, and you have read the suggested literature, you can start your work. Strategies for your growth might include the following:

- During your classroom observations and post conferences, talk with teachers about your belief in their talents and your desire to develop them further. Give them time for practice and reflection on a few strategies they can improve upon. Follow up and give more practice time in a cycle set by you and the teacher.

- Determine a list of duties held by you and/or your leadership team that could be delegated to staff members for their leadership development with support and coaching. Develop a plan to distribute these duties, based on the identified strengths of your staff, and prepare and support them in assuming these duties.

- Present your plan to develop the full potential of your people at staff meetings so that they understand the reason and benefits of the effort.

Soon, the word will be out that you are a leader interested in developing people, and that you are interested in the career aspirations and goals of teachers. The more success you have in developing people, the more successful people want to work with you. This will also build trust, as people will come to see that their growth and development is among the highest agenda items for school leaders.

DROP 3: BUILD COLLECTIVE TEACHER EFFICACY

For many years we have known about the power of teacher efficacy. Wide and varied studies have proven that beliefs matter and that when we believe we make a difference in the learning of students, we do. Conversely, when we believe we cannot make a difference in the learning of students, we do not.

Contemporary research by John Hattie, as well as William Hoy at Ohio State University, and numerous others are showing us that when teachers have a collective sense of efficacy, the result on student learning multiplies. According to Jenni Donohoo (2017), author of *Collective Teacher Efficacy*, "Amazing things happen when a school staff shares the belief that they are able to achieve collective goals and overcome challenges to impact student achievement" (p. 1). In fact, Hattie ranks collective teacher efficacy as the number one factor influencing student achievement with a 1.57 effect size. The highest of all effects in his research to date.

If your teachers do not possess a collective sense of teacher efficacy, you are missing a great opportunity to significantly improve the performance of your students. Placing emphasis and exerting energy and effort toward building this kind of efficacy among your staff is indeed justified in the research.

Get Started

Teachers will not develop a collective sense of efficacy without the deliberate effort of the leader to see that it happens. Impacting the beliefs of a group of people is no easy task, but the strategies below can help in facilitating the development of efficacious beliefs of your teachers. It is important to read current literature on the topic first. Jenni Donohoo's work provides a good foundation for understanding what collective teacher efficacy is and why it is important. It is a great book for a staff book talk to raise the awareness and understanding. The strategies below will jump start your work in this area as well.

- Build awareness on the impact of collective teacher efficacy on student learning through book talks, article reviews, and staff discussions on the research.

- Provide staff with structured, sustained, and supported instructional discussions, which engage teachers in meaningful collaboration connecting their instructional practices to the outcomes they see in student learning. In essence, send them on a treasure hunt to connect actions of adults to outcomes for students.

- Inspire group purpose and foster the development of a shared vision that focuses on a student-centered culture. Teachers develop a collective sense of efficacy when they share a moral purpose that guides their work for a greater good. In this case the greater good is improving student learning, and thus improving student's lives.

- Provide "efficacy building mastery experiences" through thoughtfully designed staff development activities. These experiences should engage teachers in discovering the instructional strategies that are working well for students and expanding these strategies across the school for greater student success and greater attribution of the success to the work they do.

- Involve teachers in school decision making in areas such as curriculum, instructional materials, professional development, communication with parents, and student-placement decisions. The greater involvement teachers have in the decisions that matter most to their work, the greater influence they feel they have on the results they are getting from students, and this builds their collective sense of efficacy.

DROP 4: USE COURAGEOUS CANDOR

When leaders complete their certification programs to become school administrators, they oftentimes do not receive critical learning opportunities to develop courageous candor in managing adults. In order for any organization to make progress on their goals, honest feedback for growth is a necessary component. But time and time again, leaders hold feedback sessions with staff and fail to get across their message for improvement. They fear hurting the feelings of the person receiving the feedback. They fear making the individual angry. They fear repercussions from the union. They fear the uncertainty of not knowing how things will turn out. They fear not being able to help the person improve.

It takes courage and practice to develop proficiency at courageous candor, but it is a mandatory skill for all people in leadership positions. How many times have you held a feedback session with a staff member and struggled with the message you want to give? How many times have you sat in your empty office at the conclusion of the session and thought, "I wish I had said . . ." It takes will, determination, courage and skill to be candid with feedback that results in growth for the individual you are working with. If your feedback to teachers does not result in improved practice in the classroom, then a different approach to feedback is needed.

Get Started

Developing courageous candor takes time and practice, lots of practice. But one thing is for sure, if you don't push yourself to try it, you will never improve your ability to do it. To get started, try the following strategies:

- After making a classroom observation, write out the two to three unedited, unfiltered points you would like to make during the feedback conference. Then work with a trusted colleague or coach to refine the points for the conversation using nonjudgmental, specific evidence from the lesson to guide the conversation. Be careful not to lose the intent of the message in your refinement process.

- As you begin the feedback session, engage the teacher in a dialogue about her goals for the lesson and what she saw happening with students during the lesson.

- As the session progresses, state your intentions. Your intention should be to build capacity, foster growth, and bring on improvement.

- Clarity is the key to candor. Clarity around effective practices and helpful suggestions to strengthen effectiveness is part of courageous candor. Be prepared to share a few key practices for the teacher to try if she cannot generate her own next steps as you talk.

- Remember that giving feedback is a dialogue, not a monologue. The individual should have time to share, process, question, and respond to the feedback. If you have been clear about your major points and have specific nonjudgmental evidence to make these points, you should be able to respond effectively in a two-way conversation.

- Don't get discouraged if things do not go as you intend in the beginning. It takes practice to develop this critical skill, but the benefits make the time and effort worth it.

- After the session, review the original nonedited points you wanted to make and assess the extent to which you were able to clearly make them. Depending on your level of success, make plans for adjusting your delivery so that the points you want to make are shared clearly through effective dialogue in the next session.

DROP 5: FAIL FORWARD BY HANDLING MISTAKES WELL

Given that school systems and schools are human enterprises, mistakes can and do happen. Yet, oftentimes when mistakes occur, leaders respond as if it were unexpected. This response may cause people to fear the leader, and result in performing their daily work from a position of fear, rather than confidence and empowerment. If the culture of the school is intolerant of mistakes, the status quo will prevail, and trust will erode.

Therefore, it is important to have a process in place for how mistakes will be handled: those made by you and those made by staff members. This will enable you and your team to derive benefits from mistakes and fail forward. Until the leader recognizes that the messages they send about mistakes has a great impact on innovation and new approaches in the classroom, they will continue to struggle to get forward progress.

Get Started

Leaders who want to build trust should examine their current practices when mistakes are made. You might hold a reflective conversation with the leadership team and ask them how they see mistakes being handled and the results that follow.

Also, consider developing a set protocol for how mistakes will be handled in the future with the team. The common understanding must be that every mistake is an opportunity for team learning. Blame, threats, and consequences for mistakes rarely result in team learning and can have negative, long-term consequences not only for those who made them, but for the entire organization as well. If these practices are reflective of how you have handled mistakes in the past, it is important to signal to your staff that you are trying a new approach; an approach that will result in organizational learning and growth. The steps below will help you get started.

- Explain the protocol you will follow when mistakes are made.

- Explain your philosophy and why you want to make a shift in this regard.

- Seek feedback on the protocol for handling mistakes and make adjustments based on the feedback.

- Finalize and share your process and then stick to it.

- The first time you have an opportunity to put the new procedure into play be sure to follow the new procedures with fidelity and consistency.

Recall the research on the factors that lead to a culture of distrust. A major contributing factor is the lack of transparency and knowledge about how the leader will handle mistakes. Building trust means handling mistakes well by learning from them. If you implement the steps here, your team will support you and will anticipate the new response to mistakes. If you fail to follow through on your promise, you will have forever lost their trust and respect.

 ## ACCOUNTABILITY CUP PRACTICES

DROP 6: CREATE AN ACCOUNTABLE CULTURE

Accountability has become a dirty word in education. No Child Left Behind and subsequent state accountability systems created victims and generated a victim mentality among educators. The mandates and punishments in these systems led to victims and excuse-making, as opposed to empowered, collaborative problem solving to help move from low to higher performing.

If you scored low in creating an accountable culture, chances are that you are relating the term accountability to external accountability systems, and/or you have had negative experiences as a school facing sanctions of some sort or consequences as a result of external accountability. In a strong internally accountable culture, the opposite happens. People feel good about their work and they take responsibility for results. Empowerment and ownership are high. Consider the steps below to create an accountable culture in your school.

Get Started

Since internal accountability is the real lever to school improvement, it is important to become knowledgeable about internal accountability and the traits of highly accountable cultures.

- Gather and read articles by Richard Elmore on the power of internal accountability.

- Share your findings with key staff members and discuss possible next steps to begin building awareness about internal accountability.

- Examine the current schedule for opportunities for teachers to plan and work collaboratively to build strong relationships among them.

- Emphasize the greater good of their work and appeal to their moral purpose when building the accountable culture in your school.

- Recognize and celebrate team results over individual results.

- Read the strategies that follow in the accountability cup and add them in to strengthen your work.

DROP 7: EMBRACE PERSONAL ACCOUNTABILITY

To create an accountable culture, the leader must model the way for staff. If your scores were low in any of the practices in the accountability cup, then an examination of your own practices regarding personal accountability is in order. Staff members tend to adopt the same mindset as the leader. They watch and listen, and take cues on how to conduct themselves at work from what they see the leader doing and saying. The leader must own every result of the organization and take charge during unplanned situations. You cannot blame others, play the victim, or make excuses when things go wrong.

Personal accountability leads the way for collective accountability and can be empowering and uplifting. It enables a culture of high performance and no excuses, and it is a lever for impressive achievement results. The first steps in embracing personal accountability are below.

Get Started

First realize that a courageous leader steps up in difficult times and accepts responsibility for unfortunate situations and concentrates on a way forward for self and staff. It does not serve you well to deflect, make light of, or deny. In embracing personal accountability, consider the steps below to get started.

- Instead of worrying that bad things will happen at your school, replace that worry with anticipation and a plan. Unfortunate situations, disappointing results, and unexpected events will occur at some point during your leadership tenure. The first step in addressing these situations effectively is to expect them and have a process ready to go when they occur.

- When an unplanned situation presents itself, stay calm and resist the urge to be a victim of circumstance or place blame in others to explain it.

- Assess the situation thoroughly and be very well informed at what is being asked of you or what is required of you to handle it well.

- Explore your options and possible ways of handling it. Ask a few trusted colleagues for their thoughts.

- Think it through to the end and determine the best outcome possible.

- Act decisively and take steps that forge a path to that desired outcome.

- Avoid sharing any thoughts with staff that convey a "why me" or "we're the victims" mentality. Take the lead, accept that things are what they are, and then take your first step in solving the problem.

- When the situation is resolved or things are progressing nicely, conduct an after-action analysis to determine if you conveyed a personally accountable stance to the staff, and make adjustments in preparing for the next unplanned situation.

- Make a list of "Things to Remember Next Time," to avoid repeating the same mistakes.

DROP 8: USE RECIPROCAL ACCOUNTABILITY

One of the major issues in schools today is that teachers feel as though they are asked to implement program after program or strategy after strategy with no real understanding as to why the new program is good or why the new strategies are best for student learning. They feel the pile on effect and they have been very vocal in surveys and social media that they are expected to make constant changes without the support, guidance and time to do it well. Reciprocal accountability puts a focus on this issue and prompts leaders to provide this kind of support to staff.

In an accountable culture, the leader leverages reciprocal accountability to ensure new practices and strategies take hold in the classroom. If you scored low in this area, you may have high expectations for staff, but have missed opportunities to provide an equal level of support for staff to meet those high expectations. In short, high demand requires high support. The steps below will help you get started.

Get Started

Effective principals understand and recognize their teachers as individual learners. Each one takes a different message and different understanding away from professional learning sessions, faculty meetings, or post-observation conferences. Knowing this, it is important to develop a support plan that honors the individuality of teachers while they are learning something new or attempting to meet your high expectations. This will go a long way in creating an accountable culture in your school.

- Before introducing new expectations or new demands for classroom instruction create a thoughtful plan for success that should include the following:
  - Clear goals and targets for the teachers to work toward
  - Transparent success criteria that facilitates self and peer assessment along the way and serves as the foundation for feedback
  - Models and examples of exemplary work
  - Professional learning opportunities that include support in small groups by grade level or subject matter, whole faculty sessions, and individual learning, either online or in printed materials
  - Calibration of everyone who observes and gives feedback to teachers to ensure consistent messaging
  - Multiple opportunities for teachers to receive formative feedback
  - Individualized support and coaching based on demonstrated strengths and areas needing development
  - Helpful resources
  - Time for refinement of practices

- Once the plan to support teachers is developed, share your new expectations with the staff and share the support plan at the same meeting. This sends the message that you are holding yourself accountable to provide support to the same extent that you will hold them accountable for the new practices they are to implement.

- As the support plan is enacted, check in often with teachers to see how they are doing. Ask what challenges they are facing and what more can be done to support their efforts.

- Hold firm on your high expectations for them, but provide consistent quality support for them as they develop the skills they need to be successful.

- Provide status reports at meetings that illustrate their progress toward the goals that were set in the beginning of the effort. This will serve as a strong motivator for continued work toward the goal.

- Commend and congratulate those making progress and those doing good work.

DROP 9: BUILD COLLECTIVE ACCOUNTABILITY

People in schools where collective accountability is high accept personal responsibility for results, and they work cooperatively with others to achieve at high levels. They function as a tight knit team, and they feel obligated to one another to do their best work toward the shared goal of all students learning at high levels, regardless of the grade level or subject they teach.

If you have scored low in this area, you may be relying on directives or mandates to get people to perform their work at a high level. Unfortunately, this will not get you to a high-performance culture, and it will send your staff into compliance mode as opposed to commitment mode. Micromanagement is a morale killer and does much damage to the way people feel about their work. These feelings are paramount when building an accountable culture in your school. Collective accountability for results is a personal choice and internally driven.

The steps below will help you get started in building an accountable culture in your school where collective accountability is high and everyone owns the work and results.

In addition to modeling personal accountability, and using reciprocal accountability to form the foundation to grow collective accountability, there are other leadership actions you can take to grow collective accountability in your school.

- Make your goals of creating an accountable culture known to the staff. Explain why this is important and what it means for them and the students if you are able to collectively achieve it.

- Read and discuss articles by Richard Elmore and others that illustrate the empowering results of personal and collective accountability in schools.

- Ask the staff to assess the current culture of the school using the descriptions from the articles as a basis for the discussion.

- Reflect on your own actions as you strive to facilitate accountability in staff. Be mindful to not solve every problem or issue for staff members. Provide support and ask the right questions, but leave their issues to them to work through.

- Avoid solving the problem for them, or discounting their opinions.

- Instead, engage them in a conversation that plants the seeds of accountability for results. Take a few minutes to help them accept responsibility for solving their own problems and empower them to take control of the challenges they face, while remaining empathetic to their needs.

- Do not share how you would handle it or how you have previously been in a similar situation. This is theirs to solve and resolve.

These conversations will inspire trust and collective accountability, and ultimately risk-taking.

DROP 10: FACE THE BRUTAL FACTS

Facing the brutal facts is an act of everyday courage, and courageous leaders embrace the facts and use them as opportunities for growth, empowerment, and improvement. The brutal facts are the facts about your leadership effectiveness and the culture of the school. These facts do not typically show up in campus progress reports unless the district has committed to conducting stakeholder surveys which provide this kind of information. If you are in such a district, consider yourself fortunate.

If you scored low in this area, it is important to know that not facing the brutal facts can seriously limit your ability to move forward. Failing to see the facts, choosing to ignore the facts, or glossing over the facts leads to the loss of your credibility, the loss of trust from your staff, and the loss of an opportunity to excel. The steps below will get you started in soliciting and using brutal facts to improve your leadership and meet your goals.

Get Started

Being able to face the facts enables you to make good decisions. This requires that you build a culture of trust so that people feel free to share their true thoughts and observations on the effectiveness of your leadership and suggestions they have for improving operations. This requires that you check your ego and hear the truth from them.

You may recall that Jim Collins, author of *Good to Great* (2001), suggests four practices for leaders to create a culture where the brutal facts are shared and confronted. I have listed these practices again, as these strategies are effective in getting you started in facing and using brutal facts to guide your leadership development.

- If you are indeed seeking data about the effectiveness of your leadership, the culture of your school and/or the quality of the services offered to your students, *then leading conversations with questions, not answers, is* a good approach. You might pose questions to staff about what is working and not working in regards to your decision-making process or the quality of the support you are providing to them. The important thing to remember is to keep a calm demeanor and thank people for their candor. You will need to muster the courage to face what they tell you and make adjustments to your leadership practices.

- During discussions with staff *engage in dialogue and debate, not coercion.* Teachers and principals alike should have passionate discussions based on facts where every voice is heard, every idea is considered, and everyone is motivated to respond effectively to the current reality. You must encourage these kinds of conversations, but be careful not to direct or coerce people into it.

- When mistakes are made and things go wrong, it is important to *conduct autopsies without blame* and engage in an after-action analysis. In this way, people develop trust and confidence that mistakes are lessons to learn from. Team members assume positive intent of everyone and approach the after-action discussion from that perspective. You must ask, What could we have done differently? What should we have considered, but did not? What can we learn from this as we go forward? Leaving blame out of the conversation allows everyone to put forth their best thinking during the reflection.

- **Build in "red flag" mechanisms.** In situations that require immediate action, such as data that reveal students are not progressing, or that student safety is at risk, or where school culture is dysfunctional, a process for response to these data facilitates change. Red flag actions may be initiated by teachers, counselors, or administrators, with all staff working together to solve the most important issues for school success. This is very similar to the early warning systems many high schools use to insure on time graduation of their students.

 ## RISK-TAKING CUP PRACTICES

DROP 11: TAKE SMART RISKS

Every day is a day of calculated risk-taking for most school leaders, and courageous leaders understand that they must change to grow and that failure is part of success. A calculated risk is one that even if it does not work out as you plan, you can easily recover or quickly switch gears to minimize any negative fallout.

Taking smart risks builds your internal strength and grit. The lessons learned while taking risks lays the foundation for the next set of risks you decide to tackle. You will be better positioned for success each time risks are taken, making the next time a little less risky. With each courageous act in risk-taking, you become more knowledgeable, confident, and open to new risks for school improvement.

If you scored low in taking smart risks, you will need to ease yourself into risk-taking by being thoughtful and deliberate on the risks you chose to take first. The steps below will help you get started.

Get Started

To get started taking smart risks, take a simple approach.

- Identify a problem or situation that conventional approaches have not solved. This problem or issue requires an innovative solution, one that has not been tried before.

- Make a list of all of the untried, crazy ideas you can come up with to solve the problem.

- Put your list of ideas in a chart or spreadsheet.

- For each idea, record your thoughts and answers to the following questions:
  o If this strategy was implemented, what is the worst that could happen?
  o What do I have to lose if I go this route?
  o What are the benefits of this approach?
  o Do the benefits outweigh the consequences?
  o Will this work for students?

- Once you have recorded your responses, circle the best two solutions.

- Share your ideas with trusted colleagues or a mentor and choose the top solution from your list, given their input.

- Decision Point: Is this where you stop? Do you have the courage to go forward and actually implement your idea? Activate your courage and take a risk!

- If you decide to implement your idea, prepare for failure and success, and embrace the process as you learn and grow.

- Prepare for things to go wrong. Be flexible, continually innovate, and problem solve along the way with members of your team.

- Enjoy the process no matter how it turns out and start looking for your next smart risk!

DROP 12: LEAD WITH CORE VALUES OF EXCELLENCE, EQUITY, AND INCLUSION

Staying true to your core values and an inspired vision for the future is critical for every school principal. It serves as a North Star for you and your staff and steadies the organization during difficult times. For school leaders, core values must be student centered and include the ideals of equity, excellence, and inclusion of all students due to the growing diversity of our nation and the role that schools must play in educating our multicultural society. This takes moral courage.

If you scored low in this area, it is very important to get started in determining your core values and communicating them to the school community. When you name and proclaim your core values, you release other people to do the same. There are many on your staff who are waiting to hear this from you. Do not put yourself in a position where your team is guessing or assuming what guides your work and the decisions you make. Be transparent about your core values and stick to them in difficult times. It is the only way to lead courageously. The steps below will help you get started.

Get Started

A low score in this area is not an indication that you lack core values. It is an indication that you may not be explicitly leading with them. Use the process below in total or in part to identify, clarify and share your core values with the school community.

- Conduct informal research on core values of other educators or schools. This will get your ideas flowing for your core values.

- Conduct a brainstorming session with yourself to list your beliefs about the qualities of your students and staff. What do you believe to be true? What possibilities do you see for staff and students in the future?

- Use your brainstorm list to narrow down to three to five core values that you believe serve as the guiding light for how you do your work.

- Develop a habit of reviewing your core values daily.

- Develop a communication plan for sharing your core values. Your plan might include:
  - Posting your core values in your office for all to see
  - Putting the core values as a header or footer on communications coming from your office
  - Sharing your core values during open house, PTA meetings, and other events parents attend
  - Discussing your core values at faculty meetings, PLC meetings, and other meetings teachers attend
  - Talking about how the decisions you make are connected to your core values

- When making decisions, small or big, review your core values and use them as a filter for making decisions in accordance with them.

- Work with a trusted friend or mentor to review your decisions for alignment with your core values.

DROP 13: EMBRACE INNOVATION AND DESIGN THINKING

Innovation and design in schools is the ultimate in risk-taking, and they require courageous leadership. Leaders who are risk takers are innovators and designers of new and exciting ways to deliver school services that improve student learning. They take great pride in trying the untried and exploring new and better ways to operate their schools. They are not bound by the status quo.

If you scored low in this area you may have a difficult time seeing the possibilities for innovation because you are see changing things as being disloyal to your district. But, this is a mistake. Every district wants their school leaders to take smart risks and find innovative ways to deliver quality educational services. The steps below will set you on the right path to becoming more innovative.

Get Started

The strategy starter for this practice is based on the work of Jeff Dyer and colleagues, authors of *The Innovator's DNA: Mastering the 5 Skills of*

Disruptive Innovators (2001), which was previously discussed in Chapter 5. They suggest that innovators possess five core skills that include: associating, questioning, observing, networking, and experimenting. These skills provide a blueprint for you to begin thinking and acting in new and different ways.

- Identify several operational or process-based problems in your school that if solved would make a difference in student learning.

- Intensely observe the current processes and procedures related to this issue. Make note of every aspect and detail so that you see and understand the current operation.

- Investigate why things are being done the way they are. Ask why and what if questions of staff, central office, and other principals to learn as much as you can.

- Look at other schools and organizations who do things differently related to this issue and borrow from their innovations to create one that is right for your school.

- Speak with trusted colleagues or your leadership team about your ideas and weigh their input. Make adjustments and refine your idea accordingly.

- Further test your ideas with teachers and consider their input.

- Create an innovative solution, one that is untried, out of the box, maybe even a little radical, to address the problem.

- Pilot your new idea on a small scale. Learn and adjust as you expand the innovation to a wider group.

- Celebrate your first innovation, even if it flops, and repeat the process!

DROP 14: FEARLESSLY FOCUS ON WHAT MATTERS MOST

School leaders face a barrage of requests, problems, and issues on a daily basis. Although they have the best of intentions of spending their time on issues that matter most, they consistently find themselves putting out fires and spending the day "off focus." In order for any meaningful, sustainable work to get done, leaders must find ways to develop the courage to say no and take control of their work.

The job of the school leader is to guard their time from distractions that take them and their people off mission or focus. They have to keep the main thing the main thing. When the leader can model focus and deliberate action toward a few but powerful areas of work, then the staff will follow suit.

If you scored low in this area, you are most likely struggling to get into classrooms, attend PLC meetings and lead professional learning of teachers. You are not controlling your time, and this is frustrating. The steps below will help get you started in taking control of your time and maintain a focus on the things that matter most to student and staff learning.

Get Started

The first step in fearlessly focusing is being very clear about the leadership practices that will move your school toward the goals and vision. Be selective and choose the two to three areas that provide the most leverage and are the most meaningful to you and to your team. Consider this question as you choose:

If I could spend all day on _____, it would make all the difference in the world to improving results in my organization.

What did you put in the blank above? This might well be your area for focus.

After you have identified where your time and energy *should* be focused, do a calendar/time audit to determine exactly what percentage of your time is currently spent there. Take the total number of hours at work for a week and calculate the total number of hours for that week that you spent on the focus area. Divide the total work hours into the total hours on the focus for your percentage of time spent on the focus. Is it 20 percent, 10 percent, or less?

Next, analyze what took you off focus. Where did you spend most of your time? Create a chart like the one below to analyze your current reality for the period of 1 week.

Activity	Time Spent	Percent of My Time
Student discipline	11 hours	22%
Parent complaints	10 hours	20%
Classroom observations	4 hours	8%
E-mails	15 hours	30%
Meetings with committees	5 hours	10%
Financials	2 hours	4%
Working with teachers	3 hours	6%
Total	50 hours	100%

Now, go through the list and circle each area of work that another staff member could have handled if you had delegated it to them. How much time can you gain for your focus by developing others and sharing leadership?

Consider these strategies as well:

- Enlist the help of your secretary or assistant principal. Do they know what you want to focus your work on? Can they help you create time in your schedule to focus?

- Block times on your calendar for the focus work and enlist others to help protect the time.

- Share your calendar structure to all parties who might have been involved in pulling you off mission—teachers, parents, supervisors, etc.—and ask for their support in redirecting your time.

- Track time every week to determine if you are making progress in spending more time each week on work that matters most.

- Make adjustments as needed.

DROP 15: MODEL RESILIENCY

Leading courageously in times of increased accountability can be daunting for even the most experienced school leaders. There is no question that frustration, disappointment, and disillusionment can creep into your psyche. It is very hard to maintain a composed demeanor and bounce back quickly during difficult times. But, this is a critical skill of a courageous leader.

If you scored low in this area, keep in mind that resilience is a learned trait, not a natural one. You can indeed develop resilience through practice and intentional effort. You have to become extremely self-aware and recognize what triggers disappointment and frustration, and then develop internal controls to moderate those feelings. Staff members take their cues from you on how to best respond to disappointments and failures. They will bounce back if they see you bounce back. A courageous leader understands this and can muster the strength to set the example for their teams. The steps below will help you get started.

Get Started

To get started on building your resiliency, it is important to know what it looks like when done well. Think of a leader you know who remains positive and optimistic even in the face of challenges and/or disappointments. They know just the right things to say to help team members accept and move on from disappointments. They are able to inspire action toward the goal even after failed attempts. This is a person you want to talk with and learn from. Ask this person how they are able to keep things in perspective and what techniques they use to model resiliency to their teams. Research shows us that optimistic leaders get much better results than pessimistic ones. Leaders with a positive outlook are likely to get the same from their people.

In addition to talking to the person who serves as your model of resilient leadership, confide in a trusted colleague that you are working to strengthen your resiliency. Ask this person to monitor your responses to disappointments and provide you feedback on how you come across to the staff. This action requires courage to open yourself up to scrutiny.

Finally, take a proactive approach to modeling resiliency for your team by predicting or anticipating disappointments and failures and planning your response to them before they happen. Anticipating disappointments can help prepare you to respond with resilience and thus model for your team and develop a resilient culture.

In summary, the strategy starters here can be used as part of your informal personal improvement effort or in a more formal and purposeful practice plan to develop everyday courage, it is my hope that you discovered a few strategies that will work for you as you strive to lead more courageously.

In the next section, you will find a simple template for building a purposeful practice plan. You can input the strategies I have shared or create your own. Keep in mind the aspect of effective practice that I shared in Chapter 6, and incorporate them into your plan to ensure that you engage in the right kind of practice, the right way as suggested by the research by Anders Ericsson.

Purposeful Practice Plan Template

School Leader's Name and Position:

School Year:

Cup of Courage Target Area:

Practice or Drop Target:

Rationale: Why is the target worth pursuing?

Leadership Growth Goal(s): Describe what you expect to know or be able to do as a result of this professional learning effort.

Desired Impact: What do you hope will result from implementing the plan?

Plan of Action: A description or listing of the actions you will take to accomplish your growth goal.

Progress Points: How will you know you are making progress toward the goal?

Completed Sample

Purposeful Practice Plan: Sample

School Leader's Name and Position: John Smith
Principal, American Middle School

School Year: 2016/17

Cup of Courage Target Area: Trust

Practice or Drop Target: Building Collective Teacher Efficacy

Rationale: Why is the target worth pursuing?

According to research in *Visible Learning* by John Hattie, and other researchers from Ohio State, William & Mary, and other institutions, collective teacher efficacy is the number one influence of all influences on student learning. It is more influential than student demographics, home life, or any of the influences from outside the school. My school does not demonstrate a strong collective sense of efficacy. There are *individuals* who demonstrate a strong sense of efficacy, but we do not as a collective team, have a strong sense of efficacy, based on my observations.

Leadership Growth Goal(s): Describe what you expect to know or be able to do as a result of this professional learning effort.

As a result of engaging in purposeful practice in this area, my goal is to deepen my overall knowledge of collective teacher efficacy, as well as learning how to

- Measure the level of collective teacher efficacy on my campus

- Use the data to develop a plan to strengthen and deepen levels of collective efficacy

- Make collective teacher efficacy an integral part of my daily work

- Leverage collective teacher efficacy to improve student learning

Desired Impact: What do you hope will result from implementing the plan?

As a result of fully implementing my practice plan, I hope my practices result in

- Deeper knowledge of staff about collective teacher efficacy and full campus engagement in strengthening collective efficacy among faculty

- Improved teamwork and collaboration for improved teaching practices

- Staff attribution of results to actions of adults (causal attribution)

- Collective accountability and ownership for results

Plan of Action: A description or listing of the actions you will take to accomplish your growth goal.

- Conduct research on collective teacher efficacy. Initially read the following
  a. *Collective Teacher Efficacy*, Donohoo
  b. *Trust Matters*, Tschannen-Moran
  c. Various articles and research, Ells, Hoy, & Goddard, etc.
- Prepare and deliver PD sessions with all staff to build awareness.
- Administer a reliable survey to staff to measure current levels of collective efficacy: Wayne Hoy Ohio State survey or Megan Tschannen-Moran William & Mary survey (both available online).
- Discuss and analyze the data with the Leadership Team.
- Reflect on current leadership practices that precede the data.
- Prepare and present the results to the staff and seek their input and thoughts about how to proceed in strengthening collective efficacy on our campus.
- Develop a PD plan with teacher leaders which reflects the research on building collective teacher efficacy (focuses on mastery experiences, vicarious experiences, social persuasion, and attitude/climate factors).
- Attend PLC meetings to model positive causal attributions when student data are examined.
- Have successful teachers present cause/effect data whenever possible to whole staff.
- Administer post survey after 1st semester to measure progress on the level of collective teacher efficacy on campus

Progress Points: How will you know you are making progress toward the goal?

I can measure my progress or success toward the goal by monitoring and looking for the following indicators:

- Teachers begin to attribute results to actions of adults as opposed to factors from the home-causal attribution.
- Increased ownership and collaboration for results schoolwide
- Increases in collective efficacy on the post-survey
- Circulation of best practices evident in classrooms
- Improved student learning outcomes on formative and summative assessments

Final Thoughts

Courage is contagious.

When a brave man takes a stand, the spines of others are often stiffened.

—Billy Graham

This book was not focused on educational heroes or acts of heroism, although we have many examples of principal heroes to celebrate. Rather, this book focused on everyday courage, which is the kind of courage that school leaders must activate every day to conquer their challenges and improve their schools for all students. If we expect the nation's principals to succeed, we must start a national conversation about the importance of courageous leadership and support our leaders in their efforts to develop their courage to lead. Oftentimes, principals are not set up to succeed, and many times, they are set up to fail because they have not had quality training or thoughtful planned experiences along the way to the principalship.

If we examine the requirements in the PSEL standards discussed earlier, it is easy to explain why a national conversation on leadership courage is necessary. An emphasis on social justice, equity, and inclusion for all students is clear, as well as a focus on each student's academic success and overall well-being. Doing what is right and just for all students and protecting those who are often marginalized, along with providing the moral direction for the school, requires the kind of everyday courage discussed throughout this book.

You may recall I started the book with three guiding principles upon which the book was written. These guiding principles are tightly aligned to the emerging national requirements for educational leaders. The principles were

- Leaders must have the courage to lead an agenda based on equity, excellence, and inclusion for all students.

- Courage is a learned trait and can be developed and strengthened with the right mindset and practice.

- Strong instructional leadership and school improvement requires everyday courage.

Through these guiding principles, and the text that followed, I endeavored to reconnect you with the courage you already have, and reignite your passion, joy, and perseverance to lead your schools to success. I hoped that the book would serve as a courage activator by bringing to light the four types of courage necessary for school leaders; moral courage, intellectual courage, empathetic courage, and disciplined courage. I also hoped that creating a framework using the four types of courage as the foundation would provide an organizational structure that would illustrate the essential practices of courageous leadership in the areas of building trust, creating an accountable culture, and taking risks.

I endeavored to make clear that courage is a learned behavior, not a natural-born gift, and anyone wanting to lead courageously could learn to do so through intentional effort and action. Courage is in the brain, not the heart, as proven by a number of studies shared throughout this book. You are in control of your own courageous behavior. I challenge you to activate your everyday courage by applying the strategies you learned in the book to quiet your fears by growing a courage mindset. You can eliminate feelings of inadequacy, doubt, and helplessness by taking courageous action toward a worthy goal. You can effectively lead instruction, build trust, create an accountable culture, and take smart risks to move your school forward by leveraging the everyday courage you have within, and engaging in intense, purposeful practice on the courageous practices that you do not have yet. Your teachers and students are counting on it and will support and respect you as you provide a model of courageous leadership for them to follow.

I will close the book with three of my favorite quotes on courage. As you read them, reflect on your work as a school leader and let them inspire you to lead courageously every day!

Frances Ford Coppola: "You have to really be courageous about your instincts and your ideas. Otherwise you'll just knuckle under, and things that might have been memorable will be lost."

Michelle Obama: "You may not always have a comfortable life and you will not always be able to solve all of the world's problems at once, but don't ever underestimate the importance you can have because history has shown us that courage can be contagious and hope can take on a life of its own."

Jane Goodall: "My mother always taught us that if people don't agree with you, the important thing is to listen to them. But if you've listened to them carefully and you still think that you're right, then you must have the courage of your convictions."

References

Bandura, A. (1993). Perceived self-efficacy in cognitive development and functioning. *Educational Psychologist, 28,* 117–148.

Beard, A. (2013, May). Life's work: An Interview with Maya Angelou. *Harvard Business Review.*

Brafford, B. (2003). *The problem of courage.* Ashbrook Statesmanship Thesis. Ohio.

Collins, J. (2001). *From good to great.* New York, NY: Harper Collins.

Colvin, G. (2009) *Talent is overrated: What really separates world-class performers from everybody else.* New York, NY: Penguin Books.

Cook-Harvey, C. M., & Stosich, E. L. (2016). *Redesigning school accountability and support: Progress in pioneering states.* Stanford, CA: Learning Policy Institute and Stanford Center for Opportunity Policy in Education.

Cottrell, D., & Harvey, E. (2004). *Leadership courage: Leadership strategies for individuals and organizational success.* Flower Mound, TX: Performance Systems Corporation.

The Critical Thinking Community. (n.d.). Valuable intellectual traits. Retrieved from www.criticalthinking.org/pages/valuable-intellectual-traits/528

Donohoo, J. (2016, April 7). Collective efficacy: Together we can make a difference. Corwin Connect.

Donohoo, J. (2017). *Teacher efficacy: How educators' beliefs impact student learning.* Thousand Oaks, CA: Corwin.

Drago-Severson, E. (2004). *Helping teachers learn: Principal leadership for adult growth and development.* Thousand Oaks, CA: Corwin.

Drago-Severson, E. (2009). *Leading adult learning: Supporting adult development in our schools.* Thousand Oaks, CA: Corwin.

Dweck, C. (2006). *Mindset: The new psychology of success.* New York, NY: Random House Publishing.

Dyer, J., Gregersen, H., & Christensen, C. (2011). *The innovator's DNA.* Boston, MA: Harvard Business Review Press.

Elmore, R. (2005). Accountable leadership. *The Educational Forum, 69,* 138–142.

Ericsson, A., & Pool, R. (2016). *Peak: Secrets from the new science of expertise.* New York, NY: Houghton Mifflin Harcourt.

Fink, S. (2011). Increasing achievement for all students: Linking central office practices to school improvement. Blog post. Retrieved July 29, 2016, from http://blog.k-12leadership.org/instructional-leadership-in-action/increasing-achievement-for-all-students-linking-central-office-practices-to-school-improvement

Ford, D. (2012). *Courage: Overcoming fear & igniting self-confidence.* New York, NY: Harpers Collins Publishers.

Fredrickson, B. (2009). *Positivity: Top-notch research reveals the 3 to 1 ratio that will change your life.* New York, NY: MJF Books.

Goleman, D. (2006). *Social intelligence: The new science of human relationships.* New York, NY: Random House.

Greitemeyer T., Osswald, S., Fischer, P., Kastenmueller, & Frey, D. (2006). Civil courage and helping concepts, and measurement. *The Journal of Positive Psychology, 2,* 115–119.

Grover, T. (1992). Distrust as a practical problem. *Journal of Social Philosophy, 23,* 52–63.

Hargreaves, A. & Fullan, M. (2012). *Professional Capital: Transforming Teaching in Every School.* New York: NY: Teachers College Press, Columbia University.

Hattie, J. (2009). *Visible learning: A Synthesis of over 800 Meta-analyses relating to achievement.* New York, NY: Routledge, Taylor, & Francis Group.

Hattie, J. (2015). *What works best in education: The politics of collaborative expertise.* Pearson Thought Series. White Paper.

Kotler, S. (2011). Courage: Working our way towards bravery. A modern examination of the real requirements of fortitude. *Psychology Today* online. Retrieved March 28, 2016, from https://www.psychologytoday.com/blog/the-playing-field/201108/courage-working-our-way-towards-bravery

Leithwood, K., Harris, A., & Hopkins, D. (2008). Seven strong claims about successful school leadership. *School Leadership and Management, 28*(1), 27–42.

Lieber, A. (2015). Joe Biden talks about courage and empathy: A unique combination. Retrieved from http://www.occasionalplanet.org/2015/09/15/joe-biden-talks-courage-empathy-unique-combination/

Lombardo, T. (2011). *Wisdom, consciousness, and the future: A collection of essays.* USA: Xlibris Corporation.

Markow, D., Macia, L., & Lee, H. (2013). The MetLife survey of the American teacher: Challenges for school leadership. MetLife, Inc.

Marzano, R., Waters, T., & McNulty, B. (2005). *School Leadership that Works.* Alexandria, VA: ASCD.

McGregor, J. (2014, May 28). Maya Angelou on leadership, courage, and the creative process. *The Washington Post.*

Mourshed, M., Chinezi, C., & Barber, M. (2010). How the world's most improved school systems keep getting better. London, UK: McKinsey & Company.

Nili, U., Goldberg, H., Weizman, A., & Dudai, Y. (2010, June 24). Fear thou not: Activity of frontal and temporal circuits in moments of real life courage. *Neuron, 66,* 949–962.

Pink, D. (2009). *Drive: The surprising truth about what motivates us.* New York, NY: Riverhead Books.

Professional Standards for Education Leaders. (2015). National Policy Board for Educational Administration.

Pury, C., & Lopez, S. (Eds.). (2010). *The psychology of courage: Modern research on an ancient virtue.* Washington, DC: American Psychological Association.

Rachman, S. J. (1983). Fear and courage among military bomb-disposal operators. *Advances in Behavior Research and Therapy,* 4, 1–87.

Richmond, R. (1999). Review: Chris Rock: Bigger & blacker. *Variety.* Retrieved from http://variety.com/1999/tv/reviews/chris-rock-bigger-blacker-1117742964/

Robinson, V. (2011). *Student-centered leadership.* San Francisco, CA: Jossey-Bass.

Robinson, V. M. J., Lloyd, C., & Rowe, K. J. (2008). The impact of educational leadership on student outcomes: An analysis of the differential effects of leadership types. *Education Administration Quarterly, 44*(5), 635–674.

Roselle, B. (2006). *Fearless leadership: Conquering your fears and the lies that drive them.* Minneapolis, MN: Leader Press.

Scott, S. (2002). *Fierce Conversations: Achieving Success at Work & in Life.* New York: Berkley Publishing Group.

Seligman, M. (2006). *Learned optimism: How to change your mind and your life.* New York, NY: Random House.

Siebert, A. (2005). *The resiliency advantage: Master change, thrive under pressure, and bounce back from setbacks.* San Francisco, CA: Berrett-Koehler Publishers.

Staver, M. (2012). *Leadership isn't for cowards: How to drive performance by challenging people and confronting problems.* Hoboken, NJ: John Wiley & Sons.

Tschannen-Moran, M. (2004). *Trust matters: Leadership for successful schools.* San Francisco, CA: Jossey-Bass.

Wallace Foundation. (2012). The school principal as leader: Guiding schools to better teaching and learning. *The Wallace Perspective.*

Warrell, M. (2009). *Find your courage: 12 acts for becoming fearless at work and in life.* New York, NY: McGraw Hill.

Williamson, M. (1992). *A return to love: Reflections on the principles of a course in miracles.* New York, NY: Harper Collins.

Worline, M. C., Wrzesniewski, A., & Rafaeli, A. (2002). Courage and work. Breaking routines to improve performance. In R. Lord, R. Klimoski, & R. Kanfer. *Emotions at work* (Ch. 9). San Francisco, CA: Jossey-Bass.

Index

distrust impact, 56–57
fail forward, 74–77, 161, 171–172
framework for, 53*f*, 141*f*
leadership practices, 53*f*, 58–77
learning activity, 60–62, 64–65, 68–69, 73–74, 76–77, 79
organizational citizenship, 57
overview, 55–56
principal profile, 60–62, 64–65, 68–69, 73–74, 76–77
research summary, 78–79
self-assessment survey, 151–153, 154–155, 161, 164–172

shared instructional vision, 59–62, 161, 164–165
Tschannen-Moran, Megan, 55

Variety, 138
Visible Learning (Hattie), 17, 164–165

Wallace Foundation, 116
Washington Post, 11
Waters, T., 116
Williamson, Marianne, 44
Worrying behavior, 133–134

A SAGE Publishing Company

Helping educators make the greatest impact

CORWIN HAS ONE MISSION: to enhance education through intentional professional learning.

We build long-term relationships with our authors, educators, clients, and associations who partner with us to develop and continuously improve the best evidence-based practices that establish and support lifelong learning.

Solutions you want. Experts you trust. Results you need.